WHEN MONKEYS FLY

Finding Wisdom in an Age of Foolishness

A Yellow Brick Road of Wise Habits
to Counter Today's Foolish Notions

When Monkeys Fly   Copyright © 2025 by W. William Haines

All rights reserved. No part of this book may be used or reproduced in any manner whatsoever without written permission. For information, contact the author at: WhenMonkeysFly.com.

First Edition

ISBN: 978-1-7358531-3-0

Clearly, we're not in Kansas anymore

PROLOG

This book is an invitation to turn off the media, ignore the politicians, and block out the devolved popular culture long enough to explore a yellow brick road of demonstrably wise habits that counter today's foolish notions:

Liberty of conscience vs Submission to cancel culture

Independence vs Serene serfdom

Self-responsibility vs The victim mindset

Questioning vs Doting acceptance of authority

Calling out the ridiculous vs Woke indoctrination

Shedding youthful notions vs Chronic naïveté

Celebrating individuality vs Identity politics

Paying attention to the real vs Screen-numbed diversion

Pursuit of purpose vs Lazy nihilism

Growing through challenge vs Learned helplessness

WHEN MONKEYS FLY

INTRODUCTION

There's no place like home, except when home is caught in a whirling tornado of foolishness. Churning like a Kansas twister, the winds of media, politics, and popular culture blow a swirling gale of blustering opinion, vaporous policies, and airy notions of every kind. All the gusty proclamations leave us wondering how we ended up in this crazy land of foolish notions, so far from the commonsense wisdom back over the rainbow. Finding such wisdom in this world seems less likely than discovering monkeys that fly.

Clearly, we're not in Kansas anymore.

This book's title is a reference to the creatures in Dorothy's dreamt Land of Oz as depicted in the well-loved Judy Garland movie: *The Wizard of Oz*. Those winged beasts ultimately kidnapped and flew Dorothy to her scary showdown with the Wicked Witch of the West. In her long journey to that moment, she traveled through a world of fanciful imaginings no less believable than many of the foolish notions that have recently been conjured up on this side of the rainbow. Yet along the road there were wise lessons to be learned, (or relearned), and these allowed Dorothy to make her way through the foolishness, returning home a bit wiser than when she left.

In similar fashion, each flight in this book offers a showdown with today's dreamy illusions, some of which are so counterproductive that one imagines that there must be a wicked witch behind them. Between takeoff and landing each flight defines a wise habit that contradicts a current foolish notion:

Ten Wise Habits to Counter Today's Foolish Notions

(1) **Think and Speak for Yourself**
Liberty of conscience vs Submission to cancel culture

(2) **Choose Freedom over Comfort**
Independence vs Serene serfdom

(3) **Own Your Outcomes**
Self-responsibility vs The victim mindset

(4) **Be Skeptical**
Questioning vs Doting acceptance of authority

(5) **Confront Fashionable Nonsense**
Calling out the ridiculous vs Woke indoctrination

(6) **Put Away Childish Things**
Shedding youthful notions vs Chronic naïveté

(7) **Treasure Individuals**
Celebrating individuality vs Identity politics

(8) **Live Consciously**
Paying attention to the real vs Screen-numbed diversion

(9) **Seek Meaning**
Pursuit of purpose vs Lazy nihilism

(10) **Embrace Adversity**
Growing through challenge vs Learned helplessness

In each theme I've tried to illustrate the contrast between the wise and the foolish using a bit of satire and some colorful analogies ranging from medieval torture to the zombie apocalypse. Each essay is a flying monkey, if you will, that intends to carry you to a little showdown of your own- confronting the assumptions sold by the media, the political class, and a devolved popular culture.

The wise words of renowned minds serve as launching points for each little voyage of wisdom, borrowed from the likes of: George Bernard Shaw, Friedrich Nietzsche, Eleanor Roosevelt, Mahatma Gandhi, Mark

Twain, Ralph Waldo Emerson, Werner Heisenberg, Jane Austin, Groucho Marx and 50 others. Unlike the Wicked Witch's minions, our flying monkeys keep good company.

But any exploration of the wise and the foolish surely first demands a definition of just what we mean by "wisdom". After all, wisdom is something to which everyone lays claim.

Allow me to offer a digest and interpretation of wisdom:

The term "wisdom" is variously defined in dictionaries. Some explain wisdom only by enumerating the acquired or innate human qualities that the word encapsulates. For example, the Oxford English dictionary declares wisdom to be: "The quality of having experience, knowledge, and good judgement". The Merriam-Webster dictionary defines it as: "ability to discern inner qualities and relationships, (or) good sense", while the American Heritage Dictionary defines it as: "The ability to discern or judge what is true, right, or lasting."

Other sources couple action to such qualities. The Collins dictionary says it is: "the ability to use your experience and knowledge in order to make sensible decisions or judgments". Dictionary.com defines wisdom as: "...knowledge of what is true or right coupled with just judgment as to action; sagacity, discernment, or insight." Perhaps most succinctly, the Macmillan dictionary defines wisdom as: "the ability to make good decisions based on knowledge and experience".

Wisdom has also long been the subject of scientific inquiry. The book: *The Scientific Study of Personal Wisdom*, (Michel Ferrari and Nic M. Weststrate) collects a range of this scientific research and serves to illustrate the diversity of thought around the topic. The editors divide the book into four sections representing distinct perspectives in scientific thought and research on wisdom, and these themes are instructive:

The first grounds the understanding of wisdom within the cognitive sciences, seeing wisdom as an "enhancement of cognition which incorporates relevance." Wisdom may simply grow from the memory of profound life experiences or may have a neurobiological basis, indicating that certain brain systems enable the expression of wise traits. Essentially, this thinking posits that the ability to think wisely is an innate capability of the human mind, (whether used by the individual or not.)

A second section of the book explores how contextual factors impact the development of wisdom, seeing it as a "real-life process" that involves the integration of often conflicting ideas. Here, perspectives are delivered that emphasize the importance of cultural, master narratives of wisdom, including religion and spirituality, or cultural influence. This is the idea that wisdom is something that is passed down through generations through both positive and negative examples, which is the process exploited by this book.

The third section focuses on the transcendent and contemplative qualities of wisdom such as are embodied within Buddhism, Sufism, and mystical Christianity. Noted in this section are the inherent paradoxes of wisdom that make it "difficult to conceptualize and measure with rigor." Here, wisdom is seen as originating outside the realm of humanity.

Clearly, wisdom doesn't emerge merely from the winds of a Kansas cyclone.

Remarkably, the final section of this scientific compendium offers an entreaty to actively cultivate wisdom rather than merely seeking to understand it. It even advocates for re-envisioning the mission of higher education around wisdom inquiry, not merely knowledge acquisition, suggesting that students should leave university not just informed on select topics, but wiser.

Quite so.

These various definitions and scientific perspectives serve both to capture essential elements of wisdom and to highlight its multi-factored complexity. Yet, despite the thoughtfulness of these explications, I think a simple analogy distills the action and impact of wisdom in a more concrete and accessible way:

Think of a connect-the-dots puzzle, the type that family restaurants print on paper placemats to keep children busy while waiting for their food. The child draws lines to connect numbered dots printed on the placemat and, when connected in proper order, the picture of a monkey emerges to the delight of the child.

I suggest that wisdom is the ability to perceive the picture that a situation's dots represent in advance of lines being drawn. Whatever neurobiological, sociological, or metaphysical basis it may have, in practical terms wisdom is the capacity to recognize the patterns that lead to good ends or to bad ends. That is a capability gained only through absorbing history's lessons and through long personal experience married to objective reasoning. The wise are able to perceive patterns in the world and the outcomes that those patterns portend because they've connected the dots of a lot of pictures over time and can see how they fit together. They have seen many similar examples directly and through allegories- patterns in behavior, in sequences of events, in broad trends, and more. The wise are thus able to act upon their understanding of where things are headed in time to avoid bad ends or to produce good ones.

By contrast, and like the child in the restaurant, the unwise simply can't connect situational dots to see the picture in advance. They either lack sufficient exposure to the patterns of wisdom (are naïve) or simply refuse to believe their eyes and instead connect the dots in whatever way will paint the picture of their presuppositions or imaginings. They are blind, or blind themselves, to the real shape of things and often try to blind others to the obvious as well. In turn, they act too late to avoid bad outcomes or behave in a fashion that actually exacerbates those outcomes. This is the opposite of wisdom: foolishness.

Still, wisdom can be acquired with the right approach. The naïve (say, a little girl from Kansas for example), can acquire wisdom through stories, examples, the instruction of elders, and through mounting experience, so long as her digestion of these things is driven by reason not emotion. That is the mistake of fools who, in search of emotional comfort, run away from the discomforting obligations of wise action. Instead of following the dots, they draw whatever picture affirms their foolish presuppositions right over the obvious dots below. And if wiser people can still perceive the monkey's pattern beneath their scribblings, the foolish are inclined to grab a fist full of crayons to blackout the picture entirely to prevent correction. **Media, politics, and popular culture are the crayons of our foolish age.**

Yet, whether or not one is able or is willing to perceive it, the monkey is right there on the paper. Wisdom lets you mentally connect the dots of situations to see how things really fit together, and that insight empowers you to take actions that will lead to better ends.

Still, wisdom does not come easily.

At the end of the movie, *The Wizard of Oz,* the good witch Glinda tells Dorothy that she could have returned home at any time by clicking the heels of her Ruby Slippers together and repeating three times: "There's no place like home." When asked why she had not explained this to Dorothy earlier (before all the trouble had been endured), Glinda blithely explained: "Because she wouldn't have believed me."

Now, if I had been Dorothy, at that moment I would have stretched out and punched that witch right in the nose, saying: "Are you kidding me! Sure, I would have been doubtful, but I would have given it a try! And, maybe, just maybe I would have avoided all the horrors that I've just been through! Did you also know about the flying monkeys? My God... flying monkeys!"

But I digress. The point is that in order to be awakened from her dreamy bubble, Dorothy needed to first gain new perspective and to practice some wise habits- even if by force of aerial simians.

As we each journey down our own road we can benefit from both the wise perspectives and the contrary lessons of our fellow travelers (whether Scarecrow, Tin Man, or Lion). But the swirling notions spun up by the media, politics, and popular culture are a constant hazard because they promote emotional, partisan, and entropic paths for fools to follow. We can easily be swept up by innumerable self-reinforcing dream bubbles that serve as little tornadoes unto themselves. These blustering echo chambers spin violently along the roadway sucking in the unaware- think: the media bubble, the university bubble, the Beltway bubble, the Hollywood bubble, political party bubbles, and cause du jour bubbles of every ilk. These intellectual blenders often proceed from premises as fanciful as Dorothy's dream. Worse, these twisters in a bubble are unlikely to pop anytime soon- perhaps not until we see monkeys fly.

Fortunately, the flying monkeys you'll find in this book are not exactly like the evil ones in the 1939 movie starring Judy Garland. Instead, these flying monkeys are more akin to their depiction within Frank Baum's original book: *The Wonderful Wizard of Oz.* At the end of that story the flying monkeys actually helped Dorothy and her friends by transporting them over land barriers to reach their final, happy destinations. This book's flying monkeys serve a similarly helpful purpose: offering high flying perspectives to let you see the forest not just the trees, or rather, the monkey not just the dots. They aim to prick the surface of tornadic presupposition bubbles that block wisdom.

No doubt you will find some of the monkey's musings to be uplifting, though others may merely raise your ire. Some may reinforce your current view while others may challenge you to rethink. I hope that's why you are here, because no amount of heal-clicking is going to let you avoid the sharp perspectives needed to burst swirling bubbles of foolishness. So be it. Though the road is yellow, it is not for the cowardly (lions excepted.)

But, like Glinda, I realize that you won't simply believe. Fortunately, convincing you about one position or another is not the point of this book anyway. Afterall, even those who study wisdom with scientific rigor disagree. Instead, it hopes to surmount the internecine tornado spun up by media, politics, and popular culture so you might consider **ten significant habits to counter current foolish notions**. They are not the only ten, but they are a good start. Just so, this road winds through quite a diverse range of topics, some bright and sunlit, and others more darkly brooding.

So, put on your ruby red slippers, watch Glinda float off in her sparkly bubble while gently pressing a tissue to her bloody nose, and keep an eye pealed for those flying monkeys. **They each carry a pin** that they use to burst the tornadic bubbles of foolishness that are in such abundance now.

We're not in Kansas anymore. You'll just have to follow the Yellow Brick Road.

CONTENTS

 *FLIGHT 1*

Think and Speak for Yourself (19)
Liberty of conscience VS Submission to cancel culture

Messy and uncomfortable as it can be at times, free thought and free speech are the sustaining power of civilization. The various stops on this flight address why all views are needed, including yours, which is why failure to keep this habit is not an option.

Medieval Torture of the Mind
Invasion of the Pod People
Virtually Tribal
Visit Hypnotic Stockholm
Of Toddlers and Bigots

Intellectual Suicide
Ideological Segregationists
The Super-Collider
Be Disagreeable
Uncivil Projectiles

 FLIGHT 2

Choose Freedom Over Comfort (47)
Independence VS Serene serfdom

When there are barbarians at the gate, we prepare for battle to prevent them from taking our freedom. Yet when authoritarians arrive at the gate to offer their services, we attentively listen to a catalog of attractive promises that will cost us our freedom. To prevent such ironic outcomes, we must keep the habit of choosing freedom over comfort.

The Unruly
No Slave to Robots
Bleeding to Death
Equality of Misery
The Pie Fight

Drifting Free
Phone Dead
Playing Monopoly
The Shell Game
The Free Market Escalator

FLIGHT 3
Own Your Outcomes (81)
Self-responsibility VS The victim mindset

Waiting for the world to make things right for you is a fool's game. It can't. The only practical response to a largely indifferent world is the habit of taking ownership of both the circumstances you didn't create and the outcomes that you must. Anything less is to be a mere passenger in a life that you should be driving.

Honkers
Tack
Mountaineering
Dirty Fingernails
Itemized Bills
Beware Ease
Safety Chains
Killing Monsters

Minding Weeds
Fixing Things
Letting Fly
No Past Future
No Biting
When Would Now to a Good Time?
24

 **FLIGHT 4**
Be Skeptical (115)
Questioning VS Doting acceptance of authority

We often find that political and social leaders, and the declarations they issue, fall rather short of expectation. To avoid falling prey to pretty platitudes and pledges we must keep the habit of challenging the presumptions on which they are based. If it sounds too good to be true, it is.

Drunk at the Wheel
The Rule of Exceptions
On the Other Hand
Shepherds

Privileged to Build Here
Lawyer-up
Runners
Dead Certain

 FLIGHT 5
Confront Fashionable Nonsense (139)
Calling out the ridiculous VS Woke indoctrination

When you feel ill-used by accepted norms it's only natural to make up some new ones. This flight examines whether we are abandoning ideas and standards for the better, or simply because the old ones recognize difficult realities that we now prefer to ignore. Knowing the difference requires the habit of confronting whatever nonsense is currently trending in the culture.

The Postmodern Abyss
Newspeak 2:
* *"Cultural Appropriation"*
* *"Democratic Socialism"*
* *"Fair"*
* *"Inequality"*
* *"... Justice"*
* *"Mansplaining"*

* *"Microagression"*
* *"... Phobic"*
* *"... Privilege"*
* *"Intersectionality"*
* *"Safe Space"*
* *"Trigger"*
* *"The ... Word"*

Self-immolation

 FLIGHT 6
Put Away Childish Things (163)
Shedding naive notions VS Chronic gullibility

When we remove the bubble-wrap encasing a delicate item it becomes subject to damage. When we remove the bubble-wrap of naïve notions we too become subject to injury, at least of the emotional kind. Yet, the habit of making full contact with the unchildish realities of life, however discomforting, is necessary in developing the opposite of naivete: Wisdom.

Of Copernicus and Youth
Fixing Flats
Failure to Molt
Passionately Incompetent
Of Pride and Pretense
Peter Pan on Campus

Theoretically Infatuated
When it's Not Academic
The Unschooled Harvest
It's Concerning
Cold Water
A Torch to Carry

 *FLIGHT 7*

Treasure Individuals (187)
Celebrating individuality VS Identity politics

Relationship, whether romantic, friend, family, colleague or other is both a center-point of life and its core source of conflict. This flight examines key elements of human nature, relationships, and the ways that we often abuse our assumptions about groups of people rather than making a habit of treasuring the individuality of those people.

Abusing Demographics
Beyond Average
Do Judge
Tight Lipped
Good for Who?
Unlovable Neighbors

The Greater Angel of Relationship
Personally Apolitical
Love of Words
Marital Glue
When "Yes" Means "Yes"
Opening Doors

 *FLIGHT 8*

Live Consciously (209)
Paying attention to the real VS Screen-numbed diversion

Every phone zombie you see walking along the street, eyes fixed only upon their screen, is testament to how disconnected we've become from authentic humanity. This flight urges the habit of regularly reconnecting with your most human self to stave off our self-made zombie apocalypse.

Spending Time with Zombies
Chewing Gum
Pull the Plug
Moo
Indigestion

Time-share Contracts
Selfie-stuck
The Price of Exhilaration
Salted Caramel

 FLIGHT 9
Seek Meaning (229)
Pursuit of purpose VS Lazy nihilism

The life lived without deep meaning cannot provide fulfillment. The life lived with meaningful purpose cannot help but deliver it. What deep meaning there is must be discovered by each of us in our own way, but that can only happen if we first make a habit of looking for it.

On Purpose
Arc of Life
Uniquely Meaningful
A Stool to Stand On
Keeping What You Give

Taking a Ride
The Atheist's Catch 22
A Serene End
A Dignified End
The Material Lens

 FLIGHT 10
Embrace Adversity (251)
Growing through challenge VS Learned helplessness

Like the three-legged dog, we have choices in our response to circumstance- to whimper in the corner or learn to run in a new way. This final flight illustrates how, ultimately, your quality of life depends largely upon how you respond to the ordinary and extraordinary challenges of life. The habit of embracing adversity lets us reshape it, rather than being shaped by it.

Whine Glasses
Losing Winners
Batter Up
Unsafe Spaces
Prepare for Courage

More of You
Getting There
Too Hard Not To
Pivot to Success
Leading Attributes

Epilogue (269)
The journey to our beginnings

BAGGAGE CLAIM (272)
- A Monkey Made Me Do It
- Flying Monkeys?
- From the Author
- Attribution
- Thanks
- Author's Quotes
- Notable Epigrams
- Index of Essays

> "In life, all good things come hard, but wisdom is the hardest to come by."
>
> *Lucille Ball*

FLIGHTS

Think and Speak for Yourself
Liberty of conscience VS Submission to cancel culture

Scarecrow, Lion, and Tin Man brought rather different perspectives to Dorothy's journey. Those differing mindsets, ambitions, strengths, and opinions all contributed greatly to the troop's ultimate success. Diversity of mind within any group, whether you are walking down a yellow brick road or tackling a difficult business, social, or personal issue is an essential factor that powers the problem-solving process and leads to new insight.

But speaking one's mind can only happen within a cultural milieu that embraces the expression of alternate points of view. Yet the foolish world on this side of the rainbow recently seems open to all forms of diversity except diversity of thought and expression.

WHEN MONKEYS FLY

Here we explore the dimensions of free speech and unimpeded thought, and why keeping the habit of thinking and speaking for yourself provides the essential fuel for civilization.

Afterall, if you and I always agree, one of us isn't needed.

Thank goodness that we're all needed.

> "Fear of serious injury alone cannot justify oppression of free speech and assembly. Men feared witches and burnt women. It is the function of speech to free men from the bondage of irrational fears."
>
> Louis D. Brandeis

Medieval Torture of the Mind

The term "medieval torture" instantly conjures images of the rack, the iron maiden, and that doctrinaire instructor from school days. Some people are so dedicated to their staunchly held orthodoxies that they believe all who fail to fall in line with their way of thinking deserve to be tortured into compliance.

In the sociopolitical realm, many quite orthodoxical beliefs emerge from distorted perceptions or fanciful theories about how to solve worldly problems. Think of the conflicts that surround race, sex, and political philosophies. Passions run high within these domains, particularly when evidence runs low. Then too, sometimes that passion is driven less by belief in the cause than for the presumably noble standing that alliance with the cause confers to the supporter.

Perceptions and motive notwithstanding, such orthodoxies frequently garner emphatic obedience from adoring acolytes who can't stand to have their beliefs questioned. So, they defend their convictions by haranguing critics and portraying them as dangerous heretics who must be both silenced and shunned for the protection of all. Later this social vilification advances to demands for legal strictures against opposition, enforced by law and penalty. The witches must be burned.

Does any of this sound familiar? If so, you've witnessed Medieval torture of the mind. Your mind.

WHEN MONKEYS FLY

Things don't advance much when the Medieval impulse prevails because it's terrifically difficult to have a reasoned discussion while being drawn and quartered. Yet the discussion and criticism of opposing ideas is the very stuff of human progress. It's how we come to understand each other, bridge gaps in perspective, and find surprising areas of agreement and places for compromise. It's how we discover that while the other person may be wrong, that doesn't make them evil. That realization helps us resist the Medieval urge to throw people into a dungeon (physical or metaphorical) when they express ideas that question our assumptions or hurt our feelings.

We thought we already had this in hand because we are the children of the Enlightenment, living in the Western world under its values of empiricism, skepticism, liberalism, and individualism. Yet that primitive Medieval impulse seems to be a deeply embedded human trait. Quite ironically, it even reared its vicious head at the very dawning of the Enlightenment within the fevered minds of the French Revolution Jacobins. They sank immediately into the Medieval impulse to destroy the structures, symbols, and people that opposed their "enlightened" views or that merely reminded them of pre-enlightenment thinking. No one and nothing was to be spared, even the very structure of the calendar by which time was marked. Thus, what had seemed to be an enlightened movement for structural change in 18th century France turned into a fanatical bloodbath at the hands of those who believed themselves to be so enlightened that their Medieval behavior was justified. We have seen this phenomenon over and over through the centuries. Our innate Medievalism is difficult to restrain.

Just so, modern-day Jacobins also operate a movement designed to shut down debate over politically charged philosophies and to stifle even the simple expression of viewpoints that conflict with their enlightened, high ground. The "cancel culture" developed so that people could be ceremoniously marched to the de-platforming guillotine if their ideas violated parochial notions of acceptable thought or use of language. The concept of "safe spaces" emerged as a kind of cloister that would protect the acolytes of popular causes from the "triggering" ideas of those with whom they disagree or consider offensive. Even on elite college campuses, enclaves that should be the bastions of the free exchange of ideas, such exchanges were often banished to the stocks of so called "free speech zones." And, in some places around the world, certain speech began to be punished with an actual trip to the contemporary dungeon of prison.

This notion that free speech is somehow dangerous signals our descent into a modern, Medieval dungeon of the mind, reducing the range of allowable thought to a mere blend of chimerical edicts and angry mob rule. Violence inevitably follows such a descent. It always has.

Yet, these Medieval thought dungeons are little more than dreamy sociopolitical thought bubbles that are airily presumed by their acolytes to hold the enlightened, progressive view. They are filled by the noxious gases of romanticized social theories, inflated by a combination of hypersensitivity, naivete, and doting compliance to anointed leaders, then pressurized to the bursting point by the force of group think.

Still, despite their taut fragility, these swirling thought bubbles prove to be rather effective as intellectual torture chambers. They exert excruciating pressure on the mind by deeming alternate views to be heretical and, thus, unconstrained discussion a punishable sin. Ironic that many of those who believe themselves to be most enlightened exhibit the most Medieval attitudes, enforcing their contentions with a ferocity that only closed minds can muster. In turn, the tortured often comply for fear that, otherwise, the torture will end only when their reputation is burned at the stake.

Again, does any of this sound familiar?

Know that there is only one escape from the Medieval thought dungeon: Never apologize for your views and continue to speak your mind despite the pressure bearing down. Know that it is the keen point wielded by clear and unafraid thinking that can puncture the taught surface of Medieval thought bubbles, but only if that clear and unafraid thinking is spoken. Every such voice has vital importance because the piercing words of each person emboldens quieter, tortured minds to assert their own clear and sharp-pointed thinking, each piercing ever more Medieval thought bubbles. And with each burst, our modern-day Jacobins are further exposed as the dungeon masters they are: a torturous remnant from the dark ages.

As more and more gassy dungeons burst, the air clears to enable breaths of actual enlightenment. But this time let us inhale not only the fine principles of empiricism, skepticism, liberalism, and individualism, but also the wisdom of ancient teachings and of practical experience. All are needed to differentiate between "enlightened" foolishness and enlightened wisdom.

It is only an unrelenting insistence that all perspectives be heard that can overcome the Medieval impulse to torture non-compliant minds... like yours.

THINK AND SPEAK FOR YOURSELF
Liberty of conscience VS Submission to cancel culture

> *"There is a thought that stops thought. That is the only thought that ought to be stopped."*
>
> Gilbert K. Chesterton

Invasion of the Pod People

Have you ever noticed that when traveling in certain places you discover a strange conformity of thinking among the populace? It pervades some institutions, communities, and even some cities or entire regions. Like the sci-fi movie classic: *Invasion of the Body Snatchers*, one gets the impression from such places that aliens had landed in the area and placed pods under everyone's bed, each containing some unearthly, mind-snatching mechanism designed to supplant independent thought. In these areas, everyone's views are curiously the same, and no one can take a joke about it.

It seems unlikely that this is the result of some invasion from space, yet the overtake often appears in dense, regional pockets suggestive of alien landing zones. In such places only certain viewpoints are tolerated, and those viewpoints are thought of by the inhabitants of the zone as the only enlightened and intelligent views. Ominously, they all seem to agree. What's more, these provincial (alien) mindsets are typically bolstered by a strong, self-reinforcement mechanism. The fellows of the pod police each other's thoughts to maintain uniform, group-think within the zone- so much so that any outsider who disagrees with the opinions of the pod will be intimidated into silence, fearing the shunning of its members or perhaps, merely out of fear that a pod will be placed under their bed!

Such locations are, effectively, alien encampments that are free only from free thought and free expression. Being ideologically homogenous they are monolithically illiberal yet, ironically, often purport to be oases of liberal thought. Alas, some are places that attract bright young minds only to have those minds steadily indoctrinated and closed to alternate thinking, ultimately losing even the humility required to take a joke about the presumptions of the pod.

Perhaps most alarmingly, once inside such an alien zone it becomes increasingly difficult for individuals to recognize the thought strictures which the pod is inflicting upon their thoughts. Thinking outside the Overton window of the pod steadily becomes, well, unthinkable- from what broadly constitutes an enlightened idea right down to what is allowed to make you laugh. Fortunately, there is a test to determine if you are currently residing in a mind-snatcher zone and you may want to take it if you have suspicions:

Tell a deeply biting joke about a prevailing attitude or position held within the zone. Have trouble coming up with one to tell? It might be too late for you. But if you can put together a firmly satirical joke and have the courage to tell it, observe the kind of reaction it gets from your regional fellows. Does it garner a knowing laugh, or instead: silence, startled offence, or a sudden change of topic? Anything short of a laugh and you are either terrible at telling jokes or are living among captive minds.

Chesterton observed: "Angels can fly because they take themselves lightly." If those around you are weighed down by humorless mono-think, perhaps it is time to take wing- before someone throws a pod under your bed.

> "The important thing about groupthink is that it works not so much by censoring dissent as by making dissent seem somehow improbable."
>
> James Surowiecki

Virtually Tribal

We sometimes think of friends who share our interests and perspectives as members of our "tribe." Such self-identification with groups is natural enough, but when tribal assignment happens outside our control the effect can be less reinforcing than it is manipulative and polarizing. Turns out, this happens to us continuously in the contemporary world.

Consider the process by which online content is automatically filtered according to your expressed or inferred preferences- sometimes called: auto curation. The algorithm filters primarily based upon your searches and items viewed, your news feed, social media feeds and posts, the ads you clicked, the comments you liked, and other factors including the behaviors of those who are programmatically deemed to be similar to you. Those similar people are invisible members of your virtual tribe.

This automatic process is designed to assure that you keep getting information, products, and opinions that mirror your current perspectives, which also serves to bring you into closer alignment with the other members of the virtual tribe to which you have been unwittingly assigned- a virtual groupthink tribe.

Yale psychologist Irving Janis defined symptoms of groupthink, notably including:

- Belief in [the] group's inherent morality
- Stereotypes of out-groups
- Self-censorship
- Illusion unanimity [belief that all agree]

- Self-appointed mind guards

Sound familiar? And what better mind guard than an algorithm?

Of course, having one's views and preferences constantly reinforced is personally satisfying. It makes us feel that we are right about things. For those on the other side of the algorithm it's rather satisfying too by making the marketing of products and policies to you and to your virtual tribe members more targeted and efficient.

But, particularly in social media, it also has the effect of exaggerating the differences among tribes. As tribal members come into more narrow tribal alignment the conflicts between tribes are overestimated, and that is the point. This amplifying of differences intensifies emotions and attention and thereby captures eyeballs- the currency of marketing products and ideas. So, the algorithms always work to constrain your virtual sphere rather than to expand it, because that's the business model.

Consider your own experience. How many of the social media interactions, news items, opinion pieces, and product offers delivered to you are tailored to suit your current perspective and interests rather than to challenge or broaden them? Moreover, even if the arbiters of your digital life do elevate a differing perspective into view, have you noticed that such views tend to be of a specific perspective rather than a diversified selection? (Just who or what is choosing that perspective, and why?)

Of course, we can diversify our choices manually, but how often do we? So, the prodding remains on autopilot, surreptitiously pushing us to remain within the confines of our virtual tribe or sometimes nudging toward perspectives of a certain ilk. AI threatens to greatly exacerbate these effects.

Groupthink is bad enough, but programmatic groupthink is insidious. The insularity it propagates within individuals and, by extension, among their virtual tribes is silently isolating and conflict inducing as virtual groupthink sets in. Of course, such tribal groupthink is not all programmatic in origin. But whatever the cause, tribal polarization is the result, and that is exactly the incendiary trend that we see growing today.

Perhaps reinforcement of lockstep accord with oneself and with like others is exactly what we don't need. Perhaps the engines of e-commerce and social media are doing us a grave disservice. Perhaps if we were to exhibit a bit less conformity with our own prior preferences and to in-tribe orthodoxies, or if we were to be so bold as to initiate cross-tribe discussions, not merely shouting matches, we could counter some of that destructive insularity and polarity. Could you not shun the autopilot for a change and establish a habit of seeking diverse ideas and perspectives on your own, even within your virtual life?

Of course, tribes, both virtual and real, will still exist regardless. But patterned groupthink need not. Dissent is possible. It takes the habit of thinking and speaking for yourself rather than merely borrowing group ideas or being unwittingly subsumed within them.

That independent thinking and choosing and speaking is a freeing process that also brings a key realization: We have far more in common with other tribes than we are led to believe. We share the essential elements of our mutual humanity- our innate desire to grow, to love, to build, and to find truth and beauty in life. We share the most important things, and as such, our tribal differences need not be so polarizing after all, be those tribes real or virtual.

> *"If you repeat a lie often enough, people will believe it, and you will even come to believe it yourself."*
>
> Joseph Goebbels

Visit Hypnotic Stockholm

Stockholm is a lovely, even hypnotic place. The syndrome that bears its name is also hypnotic, though not so lovely.

Stockholm Syndrome is a psychological phenomenon in which victims come to feel allegiance to the perpetrator of the crime against them. This syndrome has been noted in several contexts including cases of hostage-taking, abuse, human trafficking, cults, and political oppression, among others. With Stockholm Syndrome the victim comes to feel this way despite the wrong perpetrated upon them, sometimes even developing negative feelings against those who would rescue them (e.g. police.) Its name stems from a 1973 botched robbery attempt in Stockholm during which some of the hostages became sympathetic to the robbers. In hostage situations overall the syndrome appears in about 8% of such cases (FBI statistics).

No doubt that's more than you wanted to know about an obscure psychological syndrome. Here's the point: Unlikely as this phenomenon may seem, one wonders at the inventive ways that indoctrination twists our perception of circumstances, even turning reality on its head. One also wonders just how broadly this hypnotic syndrome may reach. Might this phenomenon also impact people in seemingly benign situations?

Consider a person who moves to a particular geographic area for a job. As a result of this job-motivated move he/she becomes subject to the new city's preposterously inflated housing costs, high prices and high taxes, heavy regulation, crime, overcrowding, and stifling traffic- all strongly oppressive forces that strangle the individual's lifestyle. Yet often such people ardently justify the impacts of the place that now, effectively, holds them captive. Maybe it's simply a rational cost/benefit analysis. Or maybe that person is suffering from a form of Stockholm Syndrome- twisting their perceptions in ways that serve to rationalize their circumstances.

Or consider the dedication we sometimes develop on behalf of products or companies. Once a purchase decision is made, we work assiduously to justify our purchase by seeking confirmation that our product is truly the best alternative. We find evidence that we made the right choice everywhere: every time we see the product in someone's hands or when the product's ad plays to our nodding, self-satisfied agreement with its assertions. We turn our noses up at competing products, then demonstrate ever increasing loyalty to, and advocacy for, whatever brand we bought. It's enough to warm a marketer's heart.

How many people have annoyed you with their incessant drum banging about a place, a product line, or a political party despite how obviously they have been shortchanged by their captor? While, undoubtedly, there are many factors at play in such circumstances, one wonders about the degree to which Stockholm Syndrome style hypnosis may factor into the equation.

The most sinister element of this syndrome is the social pathogen it spreads. Captives reinforce fellow captives in their mutually maladaptive perceptions as was demonstrated in the original Stockholm Syndrome case. They tend to commiserate over the justness of their captor's cause, parrot slogans, come to think of themselves as being part of an enlightened or forward-thinking group, and may start to look down upon those outside their group. They even justify oppressive force when wielded by the captor as being in the service of their mutual good. When members become each other's hypnotist, the cult-like entrancement is complete.

WHEN MONKEYS FLY

Perhaps this is extrapolating one psychological syndrome too far. Yet, this kind of entrancement clearly works to the benefit of organizations, cults, localities, political parties, and government entities (not to mention hostage takers), while remaining not so beneficial to the captives. It effectively closes their minds to the realities all around them, leaving them trapped in a self-perpetuating trance: "I love this place… This is the best product… Our position is on the right side of history… This wrong is actually a right."

Be careful to notice if any such forces are at work in your own life: unchallenged assumptions, lock-step agreement with peers, and reflexive dismissal of opposing points of view. If you detect such things, back away from your captor to take in a free breath of differing perspectives, then reconsider the journey you've been on. Time to regain the habit of thinking for yourself and expressing your thoughts apart from the group.

While Stockholm is a nice place to visit, *Stockholm Syndrome* is no vacation.

> *"Too much self-centered attitude... brings... isolation. Result: loneliness, fear, anger. The extreme self-centered attitude is the source of suffering."*
>
> Dalai Lama

Of Toddlers and Bigots

If you refuse to hear viewpoints that contradict your own, you are an ideological bigot.

If you complain that hearing such opposing points of view is somehow hurtful to you, you are an emotional toddler.

If you insist that other people must change their views without discussion so as to comply with your own, you are both.

Seems like there should be a name for such people. Suggestions?

Intellectual Suicide

It takes only a little imagination to come up with a way to commit suicide. But it takes a lack of imagination to commit intellectual suicide.

Imagination is very often spurred by the fascinating differences we have with others. Engaging over those differences requires us to compare ideas, mull over contrasts, attempt to see from the other's perspective, and argue the points of friction. In the process we often discover new insights and may come up with novel, better ways forward than either party had separately come up with- a third way, better than the other two.

But it's exhausting because it requires a blend of patience, thoughtful dialog, and imaginative invention. So, too often we simply circumvent the intellectual fatigue of it all and instead substitute a process of vote or of compromise to quickly dispatch the dispute. We ask for a show of hands to see who wins, or just nail parts of the separate perspectives together so each side gets some part of what they want. In the case of the vote, are large minority may depart the interchange dissatisfied, while in the case of compromise no one leaves satisfied. Rather than exercising imagination to come up with something better, we kill it off.

Imagination dies an indignant death under these rubrics. The process of voting on ideas, for example, offers only a kind of mob rule- the ruthless vanquishing of ideas not held by the majority. Majoritarianism suffers from the Bandwagon Fallacy- the assumption that the belief held by a majority must be true. Yet, we well know that this is very often not the case. By contrast, the process of compromise yields only the dissection of the separate ideas to piece together some Frankenstein combination. Here the Middle-Ground Fallacy is in play, which ignores the fact that one or both of the positions being combined may be completely false, resulting in a compromise that is based in large part upon falsehood. Neither approach spawns the level of discovery and imagination that can expand both sides intellectually to invent novel and better ways forward. Instead, these approaches tend to extinguish much of the good that resides within either the vanquished ideas or the surgically combined ones.

Have you not sometimes found yourself despairing about the results of a compromise or on the losing side of majority rule? At times it's enough to make you want to end it all. In such moments an intellectual suicide hotline would surely counsel a dose of thoughtful and humble dialog to bring you and your opponent back from the brink. Merely dispatching differences through some convenient device kills the imaginative thinking that's needed to find better resolutions. It's a kind of intellectual suicide pact.

Instead, keep imagination alive by actually engaging in the trying and tense discussions that you wish you could avoid. Don't simply settle for compromise or vote. Think, speak, and collaborate to find a third way of approaching the issue- the new insight that bridges opposition. Yes, it is exhausting. But doing so will suffuse your intellect, and that of your fellows, with new life. No need to call the Governor. You can issue your own stay of intellectual execution. Collaboratively invent the third way.

> "If everyone is thinking alike, then no one is thinking."
>
> Benjamin Franklin

Ideological Segregationists

Today, most people in Western countries are scrupulous about avoiding discrimination based on the demographic characteristics people possess. Except, that is, when they make it a goal to change the demographic makeup of an organization to suit their notion of what constitutes diversity. In such cases, which today are plentiful, targeted discrimination explicitly based on demographic characteristics is self-righteously rebranded as: "embracing diversity."

But a group with diverse demographic attributes offers only the look of diversity, picture book diversity if you will, whereas it is only the nonvisual form of diversity that has real substance: diversity of thought.

From an organizational standpoint, a Deloitte publication stated that: "Diversity of thought goes beyond the affirmation of equality… Diversity of thought can bring an organization three key benefits: 1. Diverse thinkers help guard against groupthink and expert overconfidence, 2. Diverse thinkers help increase the scale of new insights, and 3. Diverse thinkers help organizations identify individuals who can best tackle their most pressing problems." Maintaining a diversity of thought within any group- business, social, educational, or other strengthens that group's ability to solve problems, adjust, and innovate. By contrast, groups in which everyone pretty much thinks the same fulfill the very definition of group think. And for them, picture book diversity often provides cover for their mindset homogeneity.

Not surprisingly, many of those who argue most vehemently in favor of demographic diversity are the same people who argue emphatically against differing viewpoints within a demographic group. Particularly in politics, they tend to vilify demographic kin who hold views that differ from what is presupposed to be the "natural" views of the demographic group. They assume and even insist that everyone who looks this way must think that way. This is exactly what stereotypes are made of- beliefs about demographic groups of people that caricature and thus dehumanize the members of those groups. Such stereotypes assert that demographic attributes are what define people, not their unique minds. And here the picture book zealots reveal their quiet bigotry.

While people with differing demographic characteristics are easy to spot, discovering viewpoints requires more than a picture book understanding of humanity. It requires a great deal more curiosity, patience, and empathy. Contending with those who think differently than ourselves is taxing and can be as frustrating as it can be rewarding. So, when that effort starts to overwhelm, we tend to retire to our own group of like thinkers. But, prompted by the socially urgent drive for picture book diversity we strive to disguise the sameness of our group by recruiting those who think alike but look different. We want the appearance of diversity, not its substance.

Amplifying this superficial impulse was the DEI movement which focused on generating social and even legal pressure to create the image of diversity regardless of how it consciously discriminated against people on the basis of demographics. Form supplanted substance. Standards and meritocracy were put aside to create a picture book image of diversity despite any negative impacts on quality. Unsurprisingly, uniformity of thinking was often simultaneously enforced within such visually diverse organizations, which then also suffered from group think homogeneity.

Perhaps it's nice to have a diverse outward look, but real human diversity is diversity of mind, not body, and that real diversity brings real benefits to organizations of all kinds. So, both DEI and our own individual virtue signaling actions around diversity miss the point. It is connection with people whose thinking differs from your own that is enriching, not merely posing in a diverse looking picture book of people who think just like you.

Diverse demographics among a collection of people does not signal true diversity. In fact, it often provides cover for ideological segregationists.

> "It's only because of their stupidity that
> they're able to be so sure of themselves."
>
> *Franz Kafka*

The Super-Collider

Collisions can be very bad things- leading to broken bones, concussions, not to mention lawsuits. But when physicists use a particle collider to crash elemental particles into each other (e.g.: protons), something remarkably painless happens. New understanding of the characteristics of those particles emerges and, once in a while a new component of nature is discovered (e.g.: the Higgs Boson, discovered in 2012 at the Large Hadron Collider at CERN).

Whether in science, philosophy or everyday life, this approach is discovery at its purist, creating the opportunity to evolve from present understanding to the new by colliding things against each other to test ideas and see what happens. It is, in fact, the essential action and value of free speech, that is: the colliding of ideas against each other to see what new insights might burst forth.

Of course, in the realm of speech, personal objectives tend not to be very scientific in nature. We often don't want to merely explore the boundaries of alternate thought bubbles in an evidence-based examination of possibilities. That would run the risk of bursting our own bubble. Instead, what we really want is to have those competing bubbles crash and burn like the Hindenburg, forcing the people aboard to leap over to our bubble and to our way of thinking. Burn Hindenburg, burn.

But the scientific method never calls for the ruthless vanquishing of opposing ideas. Instead, it prompts the search for deeper understanding of the underlying principles that power such fiery collisions. In the realm of speech there is a name for this reasoned approach: dialog.

So then, who are these people who refuse to engage in the dialog that's so necessary for discovery and who, instead, merely work to reinforce the surface of their rigid thought bubble for impact?

All of us.

Which is why the default approach to differences regularly takes the form of quite unscientific, emotional argumentation and ad hominin attack rather than open-minded dialog. Of course, mutual understanding and novel discovery almost never emerge from such combative interactions. No Higgs Boson for you!

Meanwhile, back at the collider, the crashing of those elemental particles at high velocity both consumes a great deal of energy and generates a rather furious display, sometimes yielding rather startling insights. According to physicist Michio Kaku, it was a Higgs-like particle that sparked the cosmic explosion that was the Big Bang. On a somewhat smaller scale, the collisions of opposing ideas in dialog also require a lot of energy from the participants and can certainly generate their own kind of fireworks.

In this way, free speech is the super-collider of ideas. Startling as its collisions may be at times, they are essential to developing understanding of previously unfamiliar or unaccepted ideas and are the progenitors of new ones.

But it works only so long as you are willing to engage in dialog, speaking your thoughts by employing both exactitude and openness. It's the super-colliding scientific approach to communication that explodes stubborn assumptions and groupthink to reveal novel insights through its relatively painless collisions.

There is a Higgs Boson of insight out there waiting to be discovered. To find it, make a habit of using the scientific approach to differences-dialog.

> *"If I cannot drink bourbon and smoke cigars in heaven, I shall not go."*
>
> Mark Twain

Be Disagreeable

This is one piece of advice I've never had to give myself. What can I say… disagreeableness comes easily to me.

Its corollary, Agreeableness, is one of the five key personality attributes formally defined in psychology (extraversion, conscientiousness, neuroticism, openness, agreeableness.) We all have this attribute, albeit to greater or lesser degrees (some of us, much, much less.) But while being agreeable sounds like the kind of trait one would want to possess, it turns out that being overly agreeable tends to constrain self-actualization through submission to the purview of others rather than disagreeing in pursuit of one's own goals. For example, a study by the University of Notre Dame found that agreeable employees earned from 5% to 18% less than did disagreeable ones. The Agreeable, agreeably relent.

We love agreeable people because they always let those of us who are less agreeable get our way. Unfortunately, that very agreeableness can leave the Agreeable with rather disagreeable outcomes. When personal ambitions, rights, and even self-expression are surrendered to avoid disagreement, one surrenders their agency. That is a tragic loss of self, albeit agreeably relinquished.

Certainly, you should be friendly and kind to others and should not pick unnecessary fights. But it is to your distinct disadvantage to agreeably accept whatever perspective or vision others may wish to impose upon you. Make no mistake, we less agreeable types will attempt to make such impositions, setting the course of the Agreeables to our destination.

Agree to be disagreeable- at least long enough to think and speak for yourself.

Uncivil Projectiles
Recall the old saying: "He who threw the first insult instead of a rock established civilization."

Discourse, however uncivil, is preferable to violence. As such, free speech is perhaps the most foundational and sustaining power of civilization.

Place limits upon the hurling of opinions and the rocks start flying again.

LANDING

Think and Speak for Yourself
Liberty of conscience vs Submission to cancel culture

No mind is free unless it is open to the discussion of differing ideas. The free mind does not vilify opposing points of view, it engages with them to find common ground or new ground or, at least, to dialog until the best idea shows itself. The free mind does not attempt to impose speech codes, nor to censor, nor to indoctrinate- acts that tacitly admit the inferiority of one's ideas- the acts of a closed mind.

Consider your own experience. When others have worked to keep perspectives from you or to stifle yours, what was the motive? Those who place limits upon speech often proclaim that they are only looking out for the welfare of others. They are not. Their censorship is merely a grasp at control; an attempt to prevent ideas they do not like from being heard by free minds. They justify their acts by imagining themselves to be enlightened and wise protectors. That hubris blinds them to the approach of censorship's inevitable consequences- the violent backlash that it foments.

In a very practical and human way, if you and I always agree, one of us isn't needed. Dorothy's fellow travelers certainly held differing perspectives and that became the core strength of the little band as they traveled the Yellow Brick Road. So, rather than inculcating sameness, we should explore differences and the novel insights that differences reveal. Peer outside the sphere of your current group or identity bubble and be willing to test your assumptions against differing views. Then, with refreshed perspective, insist upon thinking and speaking for yourself and assure that others can do the same, regardless of whether their ideas are offensive or hurtful to your feelings. In fact, especially if they are.

The open mind is strong. Only weak minds cower from disagreement within "safe spaces" or insist upon the "cancellation" of others. In the end, failure to think and speak for yourself and to defend all others' right to do the same is to surrender your freedom, your individuality and, thereby, the essential humanity of your life. The choice is between fierce insistence upon liberty of conscience or timid submission to cancel culture. Accept the weak alternative and your life will serve only as another set of arms and legs for someone else's mind.

 *THINK AND SPEAK FOR YOURSELF*
Liberty of conscience VS Submission to cancel culture

> *"Honest disagreement is often a good sign of progress."*
>
> Mahatma Gandhi

WHEN MONKEYS FLY

Choose Freedom Over Comfort
Independence VS Serene serfdom

Dorothy never relented in her quest for freedom from the influence of the Wicked Witch, regardless how uncomfortable and frightening the green hag's attacks became. In fact, when the Wizard demanded that she bring the witch's broomstick to him, Dorothy set out to kill the Wicked Witch to secure her freedom from the Land of Oz. Strong stuff by the little girl from Kansas.

Indeed, even on our side of the rainbow, when barbarians appear at the gates, we prepare for battle to prevent them from taking our freedom. Yet we are receptive when authoritarians arrive at the gate, attentively listening to a catalog of attractive promises that will cost our freedom.

In this flight we examine the authoritarian impulse in its many forms, its deceptions, and by contrast, the human impulse for freedom.

WHEN MONKEYS FLY

To circumvent the Faustian Bargan that trades freedom for empty assurances of comfort we must keep the Kansas girl's habit of choosing freedom, regardless of how cozy the promises of eutopia may sound.

> *"If you are not acquainted with the term "useful idiot" you are likely on your way to becoming one."*

The Unruly

There are two particularly visible categories of people who always seem to dominate the policy landscape. They are hard to miss because they play off each other generating an unending narrative that is irresistible to the press. They are: 1. Those who feel compelled to rule (would be "Rulers") and: 2. Those hoping to be beneficently ruled and cared for (the "Ruled".)

The second category, the Ruled, is largely comprised of those who feel disadvantaged and so are willing to sacrifice freedoms in exchange for a promise of safety, relative comfort and, too often, to escape personal responsibility for their own success or lack thereof. By contrast, the Rulers category possesses an emphatic desire to occupy a superior, ruling position, making them the eager supporters of the attitudes of the Ruled. They believe that the Ruled must surely be in need of Rulers such as themselves.

These groups have a symbiotic relationship, not unlike that between ants and aphids wherein the aphids produce honeydew (a food source for the ants). The ants (the Rulers), wishing to preserve their food source, assume the role of caretaker for the aphids (the Ruled) by herding them into the ant shelter each night where they will be protected, but also by stripping off the aphid's wings so they can't fly away.

In humans, the food gained by the Rulers is quite a bit more intoxicating than honeydew: a heady blend of power and a claim of virtuousness. The Rulers position themselves as the ally of the Ruled by offering strong words of support and weak progressive programs that succeed only in clipping the wings of the Ruled. In so doing they inculcate learned helplessness among the Ruled who are placated through the provision of mild comfort that lacks real progress. Thus, homeostasis is maintained in this symbiotic relationship; one group gaining the safety of weak sustenance without freedom while the other gains plaudits for their good intentions. Then too, the Rulers subconsciously understand that the problems of the Ruled must never actually be solved because that would break the symbiotic balance. The Ruled might fly away. So, the Ruled are kept hanging on to that mild comfort while being made to feel incapable of taking flight themselves.

Of course, symbiotic groups such as these reject interlopers who won't comply with such a system of control and dependency. In humans those interlopers comprise a third group, one which is perceived to be an existential threat to the symbionts.

This third group, which never gains the attention of the other two, is made up of those who neither seek membership in a Ruled group nor possess the hubris to see themselves in the Ruler role. Instead, they seek independence and self-rule. Call them the "Unruly" group- unruly because they simply refuse to obey the symbiotic rules. Of course, this unruly unwillingness to comply puts them in perpetual conflict with the desires of the other two groups. *I'll just keep my independence and my wings, thank you very much.*

Consequently, the symbiotic groups work assiduously to force the Unruly into the ranks of the Ruled. Afterall, those who want to be ruled, or have been led to believe they require ruling, wish everyone to be as dominated as they. By contrast, those who wish to rule certainly don't seek challenges of their authority and claimed virtue. So, the symbiotic groups assail the Unruly by ceaselessly tearing at the core values that give them wing: freedom and self-reliance. Those values threaten the validity of the symbiotic groups' ruler/ruled dichotomy because free and

CHOOSE FREEDOM OVER COMFORT
Independence VS Serene serfdom

self-reliant people have no stomach for subservience nor desire to quash the freedom and self-reliance of others.

Of course, this ruler/ruled model has been the predominant societal paradigm until recent history- thousands of years of monarchs and totalitarian elitists setting the rules. Under that paradigm, subjugation always crushed the freedom needed for individual advancement among the Ruled, either directly or surreptitiously. With clipped wings they were never able to reach their own heights and so the flourishing they might have achieved never materialized. Even those naturally disposed to be Unruly could often be coerced to support the paradigm. They hoped that, through compliance, a wing clipping might be avoided. Of course, they succeeded only in becoming the "Useful Idiots" of the very Rulers who would ultimately take scissors to their freedoms, (a term likely coined by Lenin.)

However, in modern history the Unruly finally did manage to push aside the monarchs and totalitarians in parts of the world, including a rather unruly revolution conducted in the American colonies. In those places where freedom and self-rule were instituted, human flourishing progressively and dramatically increased in its characteristically, unruly fashion.

Still, there are those who wish to be king and who believe themselves fit for the role. While within the contemporary West, power can no longer be handed down like the crown nor easily seized by dictatorial revolution, it can be sought by manipulating the information provided to the public and, even more insidiously, through regulatory machinations conjured within the unaccountable fiefdoms of now huge, ruling government bureaucracies. Within those bureaucracies there are many ways to quietly herd the Unruly into its darkest nether regions "for their protection". Nowhere is this more evident than within the Gordian knot of EU government. The symbionts never give up.

WHEN MONKEYS FLY

Which brings us back to the vital importance of the Unruly. The continuance of freedom's blessings truly resides in their hands. Many occupy the middle class, or what is left of it. They use their freedom to offer skilled labor, to serve as business managers and entrepreneurs, to raise families, to take responsibility for themselves and for those they love, and to adhere to values that have proven their worth over time. They serve as the Atlas of human progress because without their unruly defiance of the Ruler/Ruled dichotomy we would descend into a kind of feudalism again- ants or aphids all.

Of course, the egoist Rulers and the sulky Ruled are quite discomforted by all that freedom. So, they incessantly attack the Unruly values- the wings that demonstrate how individuals may fly to their own destinations rather than forever being herded by Rulers to that nether region of "protection". Those winged values of independence and freedom are all that stand in the way of a reimposition of the old rules.

But with such strong motives, this conflict never ends. If one desperately wishes to rule, one need only make attractive, empty promises to those who would be ruled. Of course, the Ruled need only pledge fealty to the Rulers, who are more than willing to fulfill their slavish wishes. They need only take a place in the hive, shout tired slogans about equity, then wait for their allowance to arrive.

But if you wish primarily for freedom and self-rule- to hang on to your wings and attain your own heights- you must make a habit of battling the other groups with unruly diligence. Ignore the empty promises and edicts that claim to protect you from yourself and fly high under your own power. While exhausting, such unruly independence is the only way to avoid a wing-clipping.

CHOOSE FREEDOM OVER COMFORT
Independence VS Serene serfdom

> *"I am no bird; and no net ensnares me; I am a free human being with an independent will."*
>
> Charlotte Bronte

No Slave to Robots

The futurist George Gilder has suggested that Silicon Valley "tech elites," as a group, believe that artificial intelligence and robotics will ultimately bring about the obviation of human work. With the current revolution in these technologies, that forecast no longer seems farfetched and may not sound like such a bad fate anyway.

But he further suggests that those same elites also believe that a new kind of Marxism will have to be established to accommodate the social impact of such technological change. Such a neo-Marxist scheme would neuter human meritocracy by substituting a rubric for the "equitable" distribution of all that valuable AI/robotic output instead. That is: if machines do all the work, we must have a way to divvy up the proceeds among all we noncontributing humans.

But this imagined solution for technological evolution begs a question about just who or what is being served by the solution- human beings or the engines of the tech elite?

It is a notion that Marx himself would likely embrace since he too seemed to believe that the innovations occurring during his life supported his convictions about a need for structural, societal change. During the industrial revolution technology was replacing and devaluing human skill and effort in unprecedented ways. Machines were changing how things got done and industry was steadily inventing business structures and human processes to better leverage those innovations. In fact, Marx was explicit in his belief that the value of industry's output should be divvied up equitably among workers regardless of the relative contribution of each: "To each according to his needs" didn't sound like such a bad fate.

But as cheery as enforced equity may sound to some, there was nothing cheery about what actually happened in the 20th century when his notions were implemented. The nation-sized trials of the Marxist egalitarian vision which swept a significant portion of the world led to the sweeping subjugation and murderous slaughter of untold millions by Marx acolytes: Stalin, Mao, Pol Pot, Castro, and others, all of whom believed that whatever human cost must be paid to implement their utopian vision was worth it. The body count of the 20th Century Marx-inspired regimes exceeds 100,000,000 souls- lives taken not through war, but through explicit execution and wholesale starvation. Moreover, by suppressing the minds and dreams of those who were allowed to live it rendered an immeasurable loss of advancements of all kinds that those minds might have created. In the end, the Marxist experiment in equity not only stacked corpses, it proved to be astoundingly destructive and debilitating for those who survived. For all its proclamations about equity, the Marxist vision has never been humanistic. It is decidedly materialistic. It crushes the innate human impulse for self-determination, offering only the promise of an allowance for those who willingly comply and cancelation or death to those who won't.

Meanwhile, the non-Marxist nations prospered, working through shortcomings of the free-market system and ultimately lifting the level of all their people in an explosion of prosperity never before seen in the world. Then, decades later when some of the devastated Marxism-oriented nations instituted at least some free market reforms (e.g. China), economic deprivations precipitously diminished. The resulting improvement in human living standards within those states struck a sharp contrast to the disastrous outcomes under purely Marxist schemes. Alas, political subjugation generally continued within those locales with a new kind of caste system installed to keep people in the places to which "equity" assigned them.

Gilder's contemporary insight is fascinating. Undoubtedly, as in prior Marxist revolutions, many people would be anxious to take an equal portion of that valuable robotic/AI output rather than having to create value through their own efforts. Still, the thinking behind this latest incantation of Marx surely ignores two critical contemporary factors that make the imposition of the new Marxism even less likely to succeed than in the past. At risk of being Pollyannaish...

First, the 20th century Marx-inspired regimes leveraged control of media and the monitoring of speech and behavior via citizen informers to indoctrinate and silence those whose property or position was to be confiscated as part of the "equitable" distribution scheme. With a deluge of false information and stifled communication among citizens, those who had not already been swept up in the Marxist social contagion were largely blindsided by the regimes' real efforts and lacked the means for the timely coordination needed to stand up a unified resistance. An authoritarian regime peopled by devotees indoctrinated with the equity mind virus could not be effectively opposed by a shocked and uncoordinated populous.

But the availability of extraordinary communication tools and information outlets in the contemporary world would make it extremely difficult to obfuscate the intent and actions of the Marxism-minded. Word of oppressive acts could spread instantly via multiple communication vehicles, potentially spawning wide-spread and coordinated resistance. That is, unless the platforms for such communication were to have speech restrictions placed upon them by government and private entities who claim their regulation is merely designed eliminate "hate speech" and "disinformation" as defined by those same government and private entities.

Which is exactly what we see taking shape today.

Well then, let me suggest a second critical factor. In Marx's time, the free market had not yet proven its ability to enable masses of ordinary people to raise their standard of living through their own effort. The free market was extremely messy, subject to excesses, and unrestrained. But with balancing law and regulation in place, now it has. People who have witnessed how free market meritocracy affords them the ability to pursue their own personal, family, and community objectives will not willingly submit to a subjugation that sacrifices their personal aspirations to a faceless collective- regardless of how difficult it may be to compete with faceless robots.

The astounding level of income mobility within the US today illustrates free market meritocracy in action: During any 10-year period about 40% of those in the bottom income quintile will move into a higher quintile. The reverse is also true, with about 40% of those in the top income quintile moving to a lower one over the same period. And this repeats decade after decade. In a meritocratic, free market system one's outcomes are largely driven by one's ability to contribute significant value to others or, conversely, one's inability to do so. Of course, this ability to generate value increases only with effort and experience, not simply by awarding "equity" to all regardless of their contribution. The free-market trades value for value in real time, so the "rich" and the "poor" are not static castes so long as free markets operate.

However, Marxist-inspired governance explicitly seeks to lock all people into a fixed, equal caste that is overseen by a ruling caste, thus strangling the intrinsic human desire and ability to rise- perhaps through the metal hands of a robot.

Today, with the very real benefits of meritocracy in plain view, most people yearn for far more than an equal share (as if that ever materialized anyway) and will not relent to the empty promise of equity. That is, unless the advocates of the new Marxism vigorously indoctrinate the populous in the notion that "you will own nothing and will be happy".

Which is exactly the Marxist philosophy currently being promoted by The World Economic Forum and increasingly promoted by public and private entities.

This assessment is starting to sound gloomy.

But I think that there is one saving insight left. Despite the indoctrinations of the cult of equity and the hijacking of communications, some people hold fast to perhaps the essential element that defines us as humans- our existential need to take on responsibilities and to struggle under their loads as we pursue our individual goals. That desire to be the agent of one's own life and to grow throughout life in the pursuit of fulfillment, whatever fulfillment means to you, is not something that can be doled out by the hands of AI powered robots and their masters. The human spirit requires autonomy, and that cannot be replaced by automatons. So, those who understand and hold tight to their humanity will not be subjugated by the tech elite's new/old vision.

This human need is intrinsic and deep. Consider your own experience. When you have had significant responsibilities and loads to carry have you not felt valuable, empowered, and somehow more whole? But when you've experienced periods when intrinsic purpose was lacking, have you not felt depressed despite whatever physical comforts you may have had?

While the Marx devotees may be powerful, there exist a multitude of people who possess an indefatigable human spirit. This mass cadre of resourceful and wise individuals will connect the dots of emerging authoritarianism and fight back to live a fully human life- one of self-determination and individually meaningful purpose. Knowing what is known today about the deprivations of the Marxian notion, they will not slip easily into bondage. They will choose freedom over comfort, and in so doing point the way for others to do the same.

WHEN MONKEYS FLY

If these pronouncements are not merely a Pollyannaish interpretation of the human spirit, then the Neo-Marxist order which Gilder suggests is imagined by the tech elites will not come without the bloodiest fight yet seen. That enlightened cadre of sound and purposeful human spirits will work furiously and, indeed, risk their very lives to battle against the prospect of a less than fully human life powered by robots.

Will you?

CHOOSE FREEDOM OVER COMFORT
Independence VS Serene serfdom

> "The most dangerous ideas in a society are not the ones being argued, but the ones that are assumed."
>
> C. S. Lewis

Bleeding to Death

Prior to the development of modern medicine, physicians believed that bloodletting would cure disease by eliminating an overabundance of blood, restoring balance to the body's humors. Of course, this devoutly held theory never seemed to work out very well for patients, perhaps most famously in the case of George Washington who, in 1799, was likely bled to death on the theory that the bleeding would cure his severe sore throat.

No doubt, the regularly absent or disastrous results of this theory were explained away by its adherents by asserting that: *"When bleeding a patient does not cure the illness, it is only because the technique had not been implemented in quite the right way."* The advocate always believes that the theory is sound despite all evidence to the contrary.

Socialism's bleeding-heart proponents always seem to make the same claim, explaining that the reason Socialism has never worked anywhere it has been tried is simply because it has not yet been implemented in quite the right way. One would think that Socialism's several, nation-sized experiments that extended over generations have offered enough evidence to prove the system's lack of efficacy. A hundred million corpses is a lot of proof that the surrender of freedom in exchange for the promise of equity doesn't work.

WHEN MONKEYS FLY

So, when is it time to stop claiming that some new adjustment will make it all right?

When is it time to stop the bleeding?

> *"All men have equal rights, but not to equal things."*
>
> Edmund Burke

Equality of Misery

That damn Pareto Principle- the reliable maxim that 80% of results come from just 20% of contributors, based upon the work of Italian-born economist Vilfredo Pareto. It always stands stubbornly in the way of equality, with those overachieving 20%ers forever driving hard to do more and better. How can the rest of us be equal when those people always set the bar so high? It's not fair.

Of course, this intrinsic disparity in achievement stems principally from the dramatic differences in ability and in propensity to work among the population. Those with very high ability and propensity to work inevitably produce the vast majority of value within any group. Others produce value as well, though rather little by comparison (only about 20% of the total) to those damned overachievers. Yet, the outstanding innovations, solutions, and opportunities produced by those hard-driving and talented 20%ers cascade through society to the ultimate benefit of all- more cost-effective goods and services, technological marvels, work opportunities, and everyday benefits of all kinds.

These benefits only come when those who can create them have the freedom and motivation to do so. Yet, there are those who, perhaps unaware of this value cascade, merely seek equality of outcome. They work to rig the game to assure that everyone, regardless of their individual contribution, gets the same (equal) reward. They protest how the hard-driving 20%ers receive such great rewards while the lower performing 80%ers receive so much less, demanding equity in the name of fairness. Yet this attempt to slay inequality only ends up killing the Goose that lays the golden Pareto Principle (to torture a metaphor). When high-level contributors see that low-level contributors earn the same positions and rewards, they cease to produce at such a high level. Why bother?

Obviously, the insistence upon equal outcomes does not make all persons equal in the excellence of their contribution. The normal variation in contribution among us is just what the Pareto Principle describes. So, the enforcement of equal outcomes irrespective of individual contribution merely enforces a comforting lie about the nature of things. But this lie has a very discomforting outcome. It ultimately assures that no one will contribute much more than do the least of us. It starts a race to the bottom.

Still, it can be said that efforts to enforce equality of outcomes while ignoring the realities of the Pareto Principle do, in fact, achieve a level of equality. They ultimately assure an equal level of misery for all.

CHOOSE FREEDOM OVER COMFORT
Independence VS Serene serfdom

> *"A government that robs Peter to pay Paul can always depend on the support of Paul."*
>
> *George Bernard Shaw*

The Pie Fight

Who doesn't love an old-fashioned pie fight movie scene? Think of the old movie: *The Great Race* starring Jack Lemon, Natalie Wood, and Tony Curtis which featured, perhaps, the most epic pie fight of all. A hundred silly cast members smashing cream pies into the faces of other silly characters who then peel away the goo, pick up their own smushy weapon and squash it into their assailant's face. Archetypal slapstick.

In the realm of economic policy, a different kind of pie fight ensues in a competition over the apportionment of the economic pie. However, this one is carried out with rather less humor.

One philosophy of economic pie apportionment might be called the "Eat-Up" approach. It seeks to leverage the coercive power of government to assure that the slices of the economic pie are more equally distributed to all. By contrast, the "Get Baking" approach demands competition for each slice but assumes that competition between pie makers will generate an increase in the overall size of the pie and thus, proportionately bigger slices for all.

Naturally, the operating principles of the two approaches could not be more different nor more at odds. Therein lies the essential tension between these two, opposing socioeconomic philosophies and the motivation for a pie fight. Prepare for things to get messy.

In truth, the impulse behind each philosophy is the same- the impulse of self-interest. The notion of equality promulgated by the *Eat-Up* philosophy certainly sounds appealing, particularly to one who has contributed little to the making of the pie. *("If I just fill the measuring cup with cream, I should get the same sized slice as the person who bought all the ingredients, supplied the recipe, and did all the mixing and baking!"*) Government is the coercive tool that the cream measurer leverages to get a "more equal" slice of the finished product. Yet, in practice, this coercive approach always seems to devolve into factionalism, pitting one *Eat Up* group against another as each attempt to use the strongarm of government to get more of that pie. Despite protestations to the contrary, it's still a self-interested competition. The battle merely shifts to a conflict over who will control the coercive power of government rather than who can bake a bigger pie. Better have a towel at the ready.

The fact of the matter is that we'd all like more pie, and we'd like to eat it rather than smash it into other's faces. (Well, most of the time.) The real difference between the *Eat Up* and *Get Baking* approaches is in how directly more pie is pursued. Relying on the rough & tumble of the free market as the tool for increasing the overall size of the pie is diametrically opposed to the notion of equality that is enforced after it comes out of the oven. The *Get Baking* approach leverages individual liberty and exceptional incentives to drive exceptional pie makers to create exceptionally big pies. Of course, the slices vary in size according to each baker's real contribution. Yet the slices enjoyed by all just keep getting bigger due to competition between the pie makers. Just look at the explosive growth in standards of living that sprung during the industrial age when free market forces could suddenly work at scale on the pie project.

Yet this is the nature of the economic pie fight we see played out in the public dialog today. If your view of opportunity is that of a fixed pie, the argument is about who gets a comfortably sized slice. But if your view of opportunity is that of an expanding pie, the relative size of the slices matters far less than does the freedom to grow the overall size of the pie through competition. Those who say they want both simply don't understand how any of this works.

So, the opposing sides talk past each other because they work from irreconcilably different premises. But, oh, how the pies fly.

> *"These struggling tides of life that seem*
> *In wayward, aimless course to tend,*
> *Are eddies of the mighty stream*
> *That rolls to its appointed end."*
>
> William C. Bryant

Drifting Free

When technological advances and abundance give people nearly limitless options and easy comfort, they may tend to feel more adrift than free- like a ship blessed with unlimited horizons yet possessing no clear destination, bobbing aimlessly upon the ocean. Perhaps we are simply uncomfortable with such unboundedness and feel the need for grounding of some kind- reference points and edicts that lend guidance. Without a clear heading, riding the splendid but unpredictable waves just makes us seasick.

Religion once served as the ship's captain for most people, offering a moral bearing of how to live, that is: where to direct the ship. But those without religious bearings seek meaningful guidance too. Often, they find direction via secular institutions that promise a kind of moral structure of their own. One might argue the suitability of such substitutes for God, but fair enough. We have a powerful need to be guided on our journey by a captain bigger than ourselves.

Rousseau argued that societies need a religion to hold men together, contending that a "civil religion" could keep the focus on earthly matters through political unity around the state. This philosophy places government in the captain's chair for those secular ships seeking guidance. But although its power may seem God-like, this captain bears little resemblance to God. Government is merely an instrument of people which is run by people who are as flawed as we and who are as desirous of power as any other group- perhaps more so.

CHOOSE FREEDOM OVER COMFORT
Independence VS Serene serfdom

So, the contrast between these captains is stark. The God of religious doctrine defines behavioral principles that are to be adopted freely by voyagers, and which are enforced primarily through supernatural threats or promises. But the alternative god of omnipotent government coerces behavior through the force of law, enforced by people with guns.

Of course, use of that coercive force when in the defense of innocents is to the good, expressly because it takes away the freedom of offenders to protect the innocent. Less good is that fact about government power being wielded by a small group of decidedly imperfect human beings who have their own goals and ambitions. What's more, as government grows the more God-like feel the wielders of its power and the more intrusive that power becomes. While God preserves the individual freedom to choose one's heading, even if outside the bounds of His guidance, government inevitably infringes upon that freedom through regulation and law- always rationalized as being for the good of the crew. Individual freedom is progressively tossed overboard as the secular god of government progressively grows.

In a manner of speaking, we in the West float upon a ship that has the unlimited possibilities which our freedom and modern conveniences and prosperity have created. But we seek guidance about how and where to sail and look for a captain to give direction. If the captain we choose is the God of religion, we and our shipmates may freely chart and row our own course, guided by the captain's moral bearings. But if the chosen captain is merely government, the likely outcome is only a laborious seat at the oars rowing to a destination dictated by whatever Captain Bligh is in power at the time.

> "The smallest minority on earth is the individual. Those who deny individual rights cannot claim to be defenders of minorities."
>
> Ayn Rand

Phone Dead

US statistics on teen deaths due to mobile phone use while driving:

- Mobile phone distraction while driving causes 330,000 injuries and 2,600 deaths in the United States each year (Human Factors and Ergonomics Society)
- 12% of distracted drivers involved in fatal car accidents were teens. (Teen Distracted Driver Data- U.S. Department of Transportation)

Thus: 2,600 * 12%= Roughly 300 teen deaths annually in the US due to their own phone use in cars.

Modest Proposal: *"To prevent this heartbreaking tragedy we must preclude all teens from having mobile phones. The elimination of this particular freedom, albeit one that is enjoyed responsibly by tens-of-millions of teens, is a small price to pay to save the lives of dozens of other teens.*

"Never mind that those few teens might engage in other driving distractions anyway. We must take this common-sense action to prevent teen deaths by removing freedoms from every one of those tens-of-millions of law-abiding and responsible teens. They are bleeding us of our youth!"

 *CHOOSE FREEDOM OVER COMFORT*
Independence VS Serene serfdom

> "A little government and a little luck are necessary in life, but only a fool trusts either of them."
>
> P.J. O'Rourke

Playing Monopoly

Many of us have great memories of playing the famous board game, hour after hour, manipulating our properties so to as to collect ever higher rents and to dominate the board. Recall the sheer delight when an opponent landed on Park Place, that premier property on which you had smartly built a hotel.

But away from the game board, monopoly is a considerably more sober matter.

A monopoly exists when a single organization has exclusive control over a product category, industry, or another domain. We generally do not allow businesses to establish monopoly status within the economy for the very simple reason that such monopolies eliminate the ability of consumers to expeditiously switch their patronage to an alternate vendor to gain better quality, price, or service. It is competition that keeps each vendor in the free market honest because all must work continuously to best their rivals in how they serve the interests of the consumer. Consumers freely switch their consumption away from vendors that fall short until those vendors either improve or cease to exist. But without competition consumer freedom is constrained and the monopoly organization is free to charge high prices for low quality goods- expressly because consumers have no choice but to buy from it.

Is not government, then, a monopoly? Within a country there simply is no competition for its government- no alternate government to which taxpayers may expeditiously switch their (tax) payments to get better services at a better price. The control mechanism of voting offers only weak influence over this monopoly. Despite the existence of competing parties, opportunities to vote are years apart, giving politicians a very long slide before feeling any impact of customer dissatisfaction. In any case, elections have rather little impact on the momentum of huge government bureaus, (monopolies within the monopoly) that dictate policy largely insulated from the reach of voter influence, likewise operating with no competition.

Of course, within the US, Citizens do have the freedom of moving from one state to another should the policies of their current state make it uncompetitive with another in their eyes. Quite a lot of people do make such moves each year to escape regional dictates or inflated taxation but, of course, all are still subject to the federal government monopoly. Switching governments at the country level- from one country to another- is a far more disruptive and costly option.

But even that option will not exist if the proponents of global government have their way. They envision a single global government in control of all- a single monopoly of power. To see how this functions on a smaller scale, witness the EU. There, officials in Brussels make unilateral decisions concerning the lives of EU citizens yet are insulted even from the possibility that those citizens might directly vote them out. Expand such a model world-wide and it is easy to imagine how a global government's monopolistic power would steadily snuff-out the ability of Citizens to control it at all. This monopoly thing is no game.

Again, we do not allow companies to establish monopoly status within even a single industry because removing expeditious choice subjects people to the whim of those controlling the monopoly. For example, in a world with just one auto maker there would likely exist only a few model choices that suffer from rather uninspired design, mediocre quality, and little innovation, yet sold at a premium price. Of course, prior to the establishment of that automobile monopoly its prospective leaders would sincerely promise that no such thing will happen- earnestly assuring consumers that the organization has their "best interest" in mind. Yet, without competitive alternatives there would be no incentive for the company to better serve its customers, nor even to continue at preexisting levels. Monopolies inevitably serve their own interests despite lofty proclamations- because they can.

Still, we presume that government must be a monopoly and that it must be given power over an expansive scope of our lives. Naturally, government's appetite for power is insatiable because such is the appetite of the people who run it. This means that those government people will leverage any convenient cause du jour to seize greater control, promising increased comfort and safety in return, which never seems to materialize. What never fails to materialize are the ever-burgeoning regulations that strangle freedom within increasingly granular and personal aspects of citizen's lives. Over time, Park Place pops up on every square of the board, each stacked with government hotel after hotel, exacting an impossible-to-avoid cost from the players (Citizens) with every roll of the dice.

To break monopoly, control of the game board squares must be distributed among competitors. Regarding government, power must be shifted from central government to regional ones, diffusing monopolistic control. This is just the idea that was first established by the US founding fathers- decentralize government by placing power at the state level, affording individual citizens greater leverage than they would have over a distant, central government. Then too, like consumers who move their patronage to a new company, citizens also have the option to move from one region to another if their dissatisfaction continues. Which is exactly why central government works assiduously to override the power of the states, consolidating power within its monopoly at every chance.

Monopoly is fun as a game, particularly for the player who accumulates a monopoly of properties on the board. But the lessons of the game and of the free market point to the same conclusion: Government monopoly is a game that only government can win.

The Shell Game

All the free services of the internet age have led many to believe that "free" truly exists with no strings attached- an endless buffet of entertainment, communication, productivity tools and more. But free is actually a zero-sum game- like the shell game in which a pea is placed under one of three shells which are then rapidly shuffled on a tabletop while the onlooker tries to keep track of which shell contains the pea. Likewise, those hawking the notion that what they claim to offer can be provided for free move the shells around with great dexterity to confuse us about where the pea (the cost) resides. And, invariably, when they lift the shell you select, the pea isn't there. It is under a different shell.

The game is relatively benign when offering consumers free products where the cost of this "free" stuff is only the watching of advertising, or perhaps the sale of your activity data, or when it is based upon the stratagem that a free version of the product will spawn paid customers to a premium edition. But this sleight-of-hand is also perpetrated by politicians who promise the comfort of some very high-ticket "free" stuff like free college or free healthcare or even free cash. Of course, none are performing magic. What is free in one place exacts a cost in another. Thus, such high-ticket free stuff simply eliminates high-value opportunities elsewhere or mounts debt that the next generation will inherit when they lift the shell. When "free" stuff is delivered on this scale, comfort for some steals freedom from others when the bills come due.

 *CHOOSE FREEDOM OVER COMFORT*
Independence VS Serene serfdom

As such, those hawking these high-ticket gambits are merely promoting a short-sighted illusion- the notion that there will be no repercussions to the "free" scheme. We might charitably ascribe such short-sightedness to naivete. But, more likely, these are knowing, cynical attempts to extract admiration and political support from the naïve.

In the sidewalk huckster's shell game, at least you know what you are losing- the money bet on the game. But when playing the "free" game in important policy matters, we can't be sure where or when the bill will be paid, nor even its full amount.

We just hope that somebody we don't know gets stuck lifting that shell.

> *"The first lesson of economics is scarcity: there is never enough of anything to fully satisfy all those who want it. The first lesson of politics is to disregard the first lesson of economics."*
>
> Thomas Sowell

The Free Market Escalator

When we were children, we were all afraid of the escalator at first. The intimidating timing of that step onto the mechanism, the ominous rise and fall of the risers at each end, and the dizzying height of it all. The escalator is a scary thing until you become accustomed to how it works and how to use it, at which point it becomes a powerful system that enables upward climbs that would otherwise be far more difficult or impossible.

In economic terms, the free market is the escalator of prosperity. It is the powerful system that creates adaptable opportunity for all, facilitating the ascent of over two-billion people out of poverty worldwide during the last century. To wit: China explosively reduced poverty only after free market mechanisms where partly adopted.

By contrast, pure Socialism is like a staircase with a pretty façade but whose dilapidated stairs actually impede the poor as they attempt to climb. To wit: Venezuela catastrophically declined only after key, free market mechanisms where demolished.

Advocates of the Socialist staircase sometimes point to successful people riding the free market escalator to the top and sneer at them- failing to note the middle class and poor riding upward just behind them. Instead, they cry: *"Destroy the escalator and make those rich people walk the stairs!"* So, when Socialists acquire political power, they seize the free-market escalator and cut off its power supply- that is, the mechanisms that make the free market work so well: incentives, voluntary exchange, private investment, market-based pricing, etc. They

CHOOSE FREEDOM OVER COMFORT
Independence VS Serene serfdom

announce to all that the now motionless hulk is finally equitable and tell everyone to climb if they can. But over time the static stairs decay, and with so few making the journey upward there are insufficient resources to maintain even the ground on which it sits. Everything further declines.

But what of the examples of functional Socialism that Norway and Denmark provide? Despite use of the moniker: "Democratic Socialism" to describe them, these countries are in no way Socialist states, nor do they describe themselves as such. Their considerable spending on social programs is transparently fueled by their free-market economies and always has been. They have chosen freedom in their economic system to power the upward climb of people, not the empty promise of static comfort offered by socialism.

Wherever the free-market escalator runs, it enables and amplifies the effort of all who wish to fearlessly rise upward. The mechanism looks scary at first, and it may appear safer to just try plodding up motionless stairs or to simply stay at the bottom. But with a little practice, the device proves its transformational value. It empowers the free to rise, which ultimately enables increased comfort for all.

LANDING

Choose Freedom Over Comfort
Independence vs Serene serfdom

Moral Foundations Theory, as explained by Jonathan Haidt is his books: *The Righteous Mind* and *The Coddling of the American Mind*, identifies six moral dimensions upon which groups formulate their sense of morality, including:

- Care/harm
- Fairness/cheating
- Loyalty/betrayal
- Authority/subversion
- Sanctity/degradation
- Liberty/oppression

(see: moralfoundations.org)

This area of study has brilliantly provided insight into why group attitudes can differ so profoundly and so intractably. When two groups assess the importance of these moral foundations differently, their differing moral visions can place them in opposition on purely moral grounds, which they each defend with moralizing ferocity.

As one might expect, the difference is quite pronounced between the opposing sides of the political spectrum. On one side all six dimensions are similarly considered in the moral formula. On the other side, just two dimensions dominate (Caring and Fairness), while the other dimensions are thought to be significantly less unimportant or even anti-moral.

Like a blind person who might have difficulty understanding how sight could be at least as important as is hearing, those on one side of the

political spectrum simply can't see how more than two factors should count significantly in the moral calculation.

So, the opposing political sides talk past each other because their moral assessments and, thus, their goals for governance differ fundamentally. One side strives to align governance primarily around the moral dimensions of Caring and Fairness, while the other wants alignment around a fuller range of moral values. As a result, the first tends to feel more comfortable with top-down edicts so long as it believes that those impositions are built on the values of Caring and Fairness, while the second tends to reject such impositions, in part, for the inevitable repression of Liberty that comes with them, (despite declarations about how those impositions are in the spirit of Caring and Fairness.) Ironic that those who so strongly emphasize the moral values of Caring and Fairness are so apt to exhibit no caring or fairness to those who see things differently.

Consider Dorothy. She certainly appreciated the values of Caring and Fairness. But she also strongly believed in Loyalty, valued Sanctity over degradation, and fiercely sought Liberty.

Of course, we each possess our own balance of moral foundations and if Caring and Fairness is your principal focus, such is your choice. However, when authoritarian governance is installed under the banner of Caring and Fairness, it inevitably devolves into quite uncaring and unfair dictatorial rule. If the stark lessons of the 20th century have taught nothing else, they have taught us that Caring and Fairness cannot succeed as the motivation for governance without the safety mechanism of self-responsible Liberty.

For without Liberty, one day you will surely be subjugated under someone else's notion of what constitutes caring and fairness.

> *"We are at heart so profoundly anarchistic that the only form of state we can imagine living in is Utopian; and so cynical that the only Utopia we can believe in is authoritarian."*
>
> *Lionel Trilling*

 *CHOOSE FREEDOM OVER COMFORT*
Independence VS Serene serfdom

WHEN MONKEYS FLY

Own Your Outcomes
Self-responsibility VS The victim mindset

Dorothy realized that she wasn't going to get home without taking decided and diligent action toward that goal. She understood that, even in the land of Oz, waiting for the world to make things right for you is a fool's game, because it can't.

But in our foolish age, finger pointing and dodging responsibility often form a first line of defense when things don't go as planned, even when those things are the result of our own unwise choices and actions. This narcissistic impulse too often drives us to blame others, contemporary or historical events, bad luck, or virtually anything that might help avoid taking ownership of the situation. It is the contrast between self-responsibility and the victim mindset.

In this flight we explore the dots of cause and the lines of effect- the connection between the circumstances of our life and the outcomes of our resulting actions.

WHEN MONKEYS FLY

In a largely ambivalent world (on either side of the rainbow), taking ownership of both the circumstances you didn't create (say, a twister) and the outcomes that you must (a return to the loving arms of Auntie Em) is the only practical action that puts you at the wheel of your destiny.

Anything less is to sink into the victim mindset, and to own nothing.

OWN YOUR OUTCOMES
Self-responsibility VS The victim mindset

> *"Freedom makes a huge requirement of every human being. With freedom comes responsibility. For the person who is unwilling to grow up, the person who does not want to carry his own weight, this is a frightening prospect."*
>
> Eleanor Roosevelt

Honkers

When suddenly surprised and frightened by the action of another car on the road, some drivers fail to take evasive action. Instead, they just petulantly lean on their horn while simultaneously blaring the kind of facial expression that conveys a peculiar mix of alarm and entitlement. Perhaps you've noticed this expression in the rear-view mirror, or maybe in your visor mirror, always accompanied by that melodic horn. It's not road rage. It's just passive aggressiveness acting out.

Emphasis on the "passive" part, because even when life itself is on the line in a fast-moving automobile, such people don't actually do anything. Instead, they merely honk their dismay in the feverish and impotent belief that it is the other driver's responsibility to make things right for them. But it was also the other driver's responsibility not to create the dangerous situation in the first place. Honking without action only expands the threat because it places the honker's fate fully into the hands of the party that just proved itself to be incompetent or reckless. It also makes quite an annoying sound.

Honkers also proceed through life in this manner... whining about things for which they should take responsibility and action and, instead, complaining about how the fates or other people aren't making things right for them- the passive-aggressive approach to life. Somehow, they don't realize that the fates or people who have brought them to the difficulties they now experience are not going to suddenly change course to fix things. So, while their horn honking on the road is obnoxious, the whining honks expressed in daily life are simply pathetic.

Honkers in all of life's settings would do well to withhold the urge to honk and instead take ownership of both the situation and their future outcome by making a quick change of course to fix the problem at hand.

What's more, the silence would be blissful.

> *"Now is no time to think of what you do not have. Think of what you can do with that there is."*
>
> Ernest Hemmingway

Tack

Life is constantly putting headwinds in our path- sometimes mild and sometimes a gale.

When it does, tack. (The sailing technique in which a boat can sail to an upwind destination by traveling across the path of the wind in zig-zag fashion.)

While tacking does require one to travel a greater distance, it makes it possible to reach your destination, even against the wind.

Don't rage at the wind. Make use of it to achieve your outcome.

Tack.

> *"Before you can achieve any goal, you must first do the one, essential thing: Name It."*
>
> Unknown

Mountaineering

It has become trite to observe that the best thing about pursing a goal is not its attainment, but rather, what the journey toward the goal makes of you. But let's go ahead and drag that tired journey metaphor right up the side of a mountain:

You might choose to climb this mountain to reach a particular spot at the top. When you start the climb from its base, all places near the top are far away. But as you climb toward that particular spot, perhaps a landmark peak, your progress up the mountain brings all other places near the top ever closer as well. (Just don't look down.)

Acrophobia notwithstanding, you discover that the pursuit of a particular goal on life's mountain not only brings you closer to your goal, but also to all other elevated goals. The effort of the climb toward one goal builds within you the resources needed to reach any other goal too. All that climbing makes you stronger in important ways- more mentally tough, more self-aware, more emotionally resilient, more knowledgeable, more comfortable with risk, more capable of dealing with adversity, more accustomed to heights, and so on. As Viktor Frankl observed: "Even when it is not fully attained, we become better by striving for a higher goal."

These inner capabilities are built step-by-step as you exert great effort in the climb and, in turn, they make ever more possibilities available as you climb. When you pursue one elevated goal, they all get closer.

Consider your own experience. When you have strongly pursued a goal yet were ultimately unsuccessful in your pursuit, didn't you find that you saw the world and its possibilities a bit differently afterward? Didn't other possibilities appear a little closer than they had before? That was the view gained from your higher perch.

So, name a peek you'd like to attain. Just make sure you are picking a really high one and that you strive to reach it with all your might. Then, even if you fail to reach that height, or if you merely change your mind about your destination during the journey, the capabilities built through your no-excuses climbing will make every new peek far more attainable.

Besides, you'd probably look pretty sporty in those crampons.

> *"It will never rain roses: when we want to have more roses we must plant more..."*
>
> George Eliot (pen name of Mary Ann Evans)

Dirty Fingernails

If you want to grow a forest you need to plant a lot of seeds, and all that planting is going to make for some pretty dirty fingernails. Then too, many of the seeds you plant will fail to sprout, many of those that do sprout will perish as saplings and, later, many grown trees will simply die or be blown over in a storm. All this requires yet more planning just to keep up.

But if you resolve to steadily and relentlessly plant all those seeds, in twenty or thirty years you'll look past those tattered and grubby nails to see what you have created: a forest of lush, noble trees standing over a vast landscape. Such a forest forms an ecosystem that has value not just to you but also to the animals that make their home there, to the plants that thrive on the forest floor, and to the people who benefit from its beauty and shade.

Opportunity, relationships, and all forms of success start from the planting of seeds as well. These are the seeds of your talents and passions, of your thirst for knowledge, of your care giving, and risk-taking, and hard work, and more. Such seeds, when planted and nourished, grow the forest of your life, creating an ecosystem that serves everyone within its reach: your friends, family, community, and yourself. Even if you start with a limited number of seeds- the limits of your abilities, your upbringing, or the conditions of your life to date- your fledgling forest will naturally propagate new seeds. They are the seeds that emerge from your growing experience, connections, knowledge, and increasing wisdom. When you then plant and nurture those seeds your forest grows still broader.

OWN YOUR OUTCOMES
Self-responsibility VS The victim mindset

Then too, starting life with an abundance of seeds is no guarantee of a healthy forest. Those seeds must still be planted and cared for, with yet more planting required to keep up with attrition: the plans that didn't turn out as expected, the changes in circumstances, and the tragedies you could not foresee that kill-off some of your forest just when it seemed near completion. Whether starting small or large, there will be constant planting, and all that time in the soil is sure to put a lot more dirt under your nails.

So be it. As you wash your hands at the end of each planting day, celebrate the dirt under those fingernails as a reminder that this forest is entirely in your hands.

> *"It is never too late to become the person you always thought you could be."*
>
> *George Eliot*

Itemized Bills

We always consider the price for acquiring things, carefully weighing the benefits against the cost and imagining those benefits- right down to the glory of that new car smell. But we seldom seriously consider the price for not doing a thing that we know we should.

Still, there is a tiny voice in our heads that is paying attention to such trade-offs. It whispers entreaties, urging us to attend to that which should be attended to. Yet, when that inner voice tells us that we should act on some tedious matter, we often dismiss it without thoroughly considering the cost. These costs come in the forms of lost opportunity or long-term expense and, ultimately, in regret. Inaction has a price too, but it is charged on credit to be paid later. So, we push aside the prodding of that tiny voice to pursue exciting new things that we might acquire or do that will be more satisfying to our temporal emotions.

This behavior is better known as procrastination, a well-studied psychological phenomenon. In a study conducted by Laura Rabin, published in the Journal of Clinical and Experimental Neuropsychology, Rabin found that procrastination was negatively correlated with all nine clinical subscales of executive functioning: impulsivity, self-monitoring, planning and organization, activity shifting, task initiation, task monitoring, emotional control, working memory, and general orderliness. She suggested that this finding might be an "expression of subtle executive dysfunction" in people who are otherwise neuropsychologically healthy.

But don't self-diagnose and resign yourself to a life of procrastination and regrets. For most of us, the causative factors are far less clinical. As Timothy Pychyl of Carleton University suggests, the best remedy for this self-inflicted wound may be to simply forgive oneself for past evasions so you can get on with life, leveraging a bit more forethought in future.

Whatever the causation of this behavior, there are usually very tangible prices to be paid for procrastination. That inner voice in your head should be listened to like a klaxon that is sounding to alert you to a coming price: some combination of missed opportunity, loss, increased expense, or pain of some other kind. The dismaying feeling which that alarm generates can serve as motivation to actually do something about the situation, despite your reticence, despite the appealing notion that you'd be better equipped to do it later, and despite your natural inclination to minimize or rationalize the negatives. Sound familiar?

If that alarming inner voice was right, chances are that the future pain resulting from inaction is going to be far more hurtful than would be the near-term price of acting to make things as they should be. It's unlikely that you have some "subtle executive dysfunction" forcing you into procrastination. You well know that voice in your head has regularly proven itself to be annoyingly right.

Think of it this way: You always ask the price of anything before you decide to own it. You consider its value and pay what you consider to be a fair price upfront. But the results of our inaction carry a price too, though it is never a negotiated, fair price. The bill for inaction comes only after the fact, like that of the meal ordered from a menu without prices printed on it. You ordered this meal in ignorance by failing to ask the price. Now that you've eaten, it's too late. The check will come.

But unlike the restaurant bill, inaction in the face of your internal alarm can have profound impacts on who you ultimately become. The things you delay may also be the opportunities that you deny yourself. So, asking yourself to itemize the coming bill in advance lets you make

WHEN MONKEYS FLY

better choices about what you will do and will not do. It lets you better set the price you are willing to pay for the action of inaction.

OWN YOUR OUTCOMES
Self-responsibility VS The victim mindset

> *"Do something every day that you don't want to do; this is the golden rule for acquiring the habit of doing your duty without pain."*
>
> Mark Twain

Beware Ease

Treading water is a lot easier than swimming. There is none of that submerging your face in the water nor the incessant gasping for breath. You can even do it with sunglasses on, lending a rather stylish look to a rather unstylish activity.

But the stationary ease of treading water, however stylishly executed, eliminates forward progress. So, while it is certainly easier to remain afloat in one place, if you never reach a destination, sooner or later you drown.

By contrast, when you work constantly to improve, (making forward progress), things never seem to get any easier. Consider elite, Olympic athletes. These remarkable individuals find their sports to be just as challenging as novices do. This seems counter intuitive but remember that the elite athlete continuously seeks ever higher levels of performance, and those higher levels are extremely challenging to reach. In the case of Olympic swimmers, it can take months of 7-days-per-week grueling practices before athletes are able to improve their times by just tenths of a second. Still, if they want to own the gold medal, they understand they must own the effort it takes to get it, and that means the work never gets any easier for them.

Sure, the elite swimmer could just pop on his/her Ray-Ban's and casually tread water, absorbing the admiration of regular folks who can't believe how easily they stay above the surface. But eventually fatigue will set in, even if just the monstrous fatigue of boredom. At that point, all the sun-spectacled floaters will simply drown in place. Which is actually a quite unstylish end.

Reaching a worthy outcome is never easy. If suddenly things get very easy for you, it may be that you've become very good at what you do, but it also means that you've stopped making progress.

Beware of ease unless you are really, really good at holding your breath.

> "There are people, who the more you do for them, the less they will do for themselves."
>
> Jane Austin

Safety Chains

Without a safety net, the repercussions of a fall are severe. This knowledge compels us to be extraordinarily careful in our steps aloft, whether we are watching our footing, our behavior, or perhaps our income. We pay attention to what's happening and exercise discipline to avoid falls of many kinds.

But when a safety net is persistently and unconditionally available, many people are less attentive to the potential fall. They exercise less focus and discipline, and some may intentionally fall, reveling in the abandon of their plumet. Once fallen some then find that laying in that net is decidedly easier than the responsibility of walking aloft. For them it can seem appealing, or at least "safe", to simply loll in the net for a very long time rather than again taking on the responsibility of the heights.

What kind of a circus is that?

Such is the impact of the social safety net. Most citizens exercise focus and discipline to avoid a fall into its net. But some do fall and some of those find the net's relative comfort sufficient to let them remain there for a very long time. But the longer one lingers, the more the safety net transforms into a kind of chain, psychologically shackling those who have fallen into it. Safer to simply stay in the net than to risk another fall they think, the thought that transforms the safety device into a prison.

These shackles can even be handed down to the progeny of the fallers. A study by Mary Corcoran and Roger Gordon of the University of

WHEN MONKEYS FLY

Michigan found that among like families receiving some portion of their income from Welfare, those families with a greater proportion of non-welfare income during a boy's childhood were associated with higher earnings by the boy once an adult (over age 25).

If the nut doesn't fall far from the tree, perhaps we should reconsider just how soft the landing is perceived to be. Perhaps our social safety net ought to be more of a safety line instead. The safety line halts your fall with an abrupt stop as the line goes taught, preventing tragedy, but resulting in a rather uncomfortable dangle at its end. One never wants to remain dangling at the end of a safety line for long. One rushes to climb back up.

Though that dangle might seem a harsh remedy, it may be the most charitable thing to do on behalf of the faller and for future generations of would-be fallers. By spurring the faller to promptly climb again they are likely to build new strength along the way and, perhaps, new dedication to climb further still to reach a more stable perch than before.

Of course, the issues surrounding the utility of the social safety net are complex, but the principle remains. Regardless of the next height attained by the faller/climber, the mere act of climbing builds strength and creates the promise of something better... certainly better than lolling forever shackled by the impersonal chains of the safety net and passing on that impulse to one's offspring.

Whatever stops a person's fall, it is vital that they not become comfortable at the stopping point. To own a better outcome we must always start climbing again immediately.

The show must go on.

OWN YOUR OUTCOMES
Self-responsibility VS The victim mindset

> *"There is no later. This is later."*
>
> Cormac McCarthy

Killing Monsters

Small problems don't typically resolve themselves. Sure, maybe it is just a small thing. Maybe it will go away. Maybe the Good Witch of the North will step-in and take care of it for you in the nick-of-time. But probably not.

Small problems tend to grow into bigger ones by spawning other little problems that conspire to amplify their size. This phenomenon is defined as a vicious circle: "A sequence of reciprocal cause and effect in which two or more elements intensify and aggravate each other, leading inexorably to a worsening of the situation." Unbroken, the circle transforms small monsters into bigger ones that become increasingly difficult to deal with.

Perhaps it is a relationship that turned slightly the wrong way. Maybe it is that funny sound you heard in the engine compartment. It might simply be a worrisome notion about a person or a plan that is dogging you. Regardless of what it is nor how small the signal, pay attention. Assume that these little things will not go away without direct intervention and that, in fact, they will worsen. That relationship will devolve into a blow-up, that funny sound will turn into an engine rebuild, and that worry will transform into regret.

When you detect the footsteps of a tiny monster, stomp on the little bastard. Don't put it off. He'll use the time you give him to grow bigger and bigger until stomping him out is no longer an option. At that point you may be in for a real fight, perhaps one that you can no longer win.

Regardless of what it is, to own the outcome, kill the monster while it's small.

> "A great many people think they are thinking when they are merely rearranging their prejudices."
>
> William James

Minding Weeds

You stoop over the patch of flowers, sweating in the sun, rhythmically reaching down to wiggle yet another weed from the ground. You curse the little intruders. You know that if you don't pull them they will grow and grow and choke out the flowers that you so artfully planted. They must go, and you must be the one to make them go.

Our thoughts are similar in kind, always including a complement of both flowering ideas and weedy notions. But it is difficult to tell the difference between the two at first. Whether a garden weed or a weedy thought, the little sprouts can look pretty much the same when they first appear. Really terrible notions can look rather smart and appealing when they pop-up and we are encouraged to nurture them. But as such weeds grow the differences become sharper and it becomes evident that something must be done to stop their encroachment on your flowering ideals.

Of course, we are all entitled to our private thoughts however scraggly they might be. The uniqueness of our individual contributions stem partly from private thoughts that might look pretty weedy from the outside. Some flowers need to mature before their potential can be seen, and it is fair to tend them in the privacy of our minds as they do. But we also tend to entertain some pretty weedy thoughts that obviously should not be allowed to grow: "They wouldn't even notice if I did it."; "I should get even with him!"; "What she doesn't know won't hurt her." etc.

Typically, when we tolerate such weedy notions, we comfort ourselves with a belief that they are merely entertaining thoughts that we'd never act upon. But such thoughts are not static. Left to grow in your mental garden they become ever more firmly rooted, familiar, and comfortable. Then, with strong roots they inevitably sprout other weedy thoughts of the same variety. Your increasing tolerance for such varieties means that the new spouts will also grow and propagate. With ever less space for your flowering ideals and increasing comfort with weedy thoughts, the things that you told yourself would never be acted upon grow ever closer to emerging in the world at your hand. The ancient Chinese philosopher Laozi put it this way: "Watch your thoughts, they become words. Watch your words, they become actions…"

As in any garden, there is only one way to deal with weeds in the mental garden of your mind. Remove the weedy thoughts that will doubtlessly choke the roots of your best intentions, while nurturing the flowering thoughts that can lead to the kind of outcomes that your highest ambition seeks. This weeding is a simple practice of thinking about the kinds of things that the person you wish to be would think about, while eliminating thoughts about the kinds of things that the person you don't wish to be would think about.

Simple? Yes. Easy? Certainly not. A good start is to catalog just what is growing in your mind, both weeds and flowers. Doubtlessly, you have some of both. The list makes you aware of just what needs to be removed and what you want to flower. It enables the first step in weeding your mental garden- noticing when a weedy thought crops up.

To pull that weed, switch your thoughts away from the weedy one to a flowering one that you would prefer to grow in its place. Replacement is removal in the garden of your mind. Of course, the weedy thought will try to sprout again from whatever root was left behind, so the process must be repeated just like in your yard. But each yank leaves the weedy thought weaker than before and easier to pluck the next time it pokes above the surface.

Mind the weeds and your mental garden will become a cascade of thoughts about the better life you envision rather than a tangled riot of exactly what you don't want. Do it consistently and those better thoughts will turn into acts that will make your vision a reality.

Fixing Things

We seem to possess an innate impulse to deny or obfuscate the wrongs we commit. More than just face saving, it is an attempt to convince both others and ourselves that we are the good people that we believe ourselves to be, despite evidence to the contrary. And so, we tell little lies about the circumstances of the situation in which we misused people or property, or we bring up examples of others who committed worse offences that make us look good by comparison, or sometimes pretend that we were completely unaware that our actions had caused injury at all. We can be endlessly inventive when our reputation is at stake.

But if instead of rationalizing we simply acknowledge the wrong we have committed, we can change our course from deception to redemption. That process starts by asking a simple question: "What can now do to fix it?" Asked with sincere intent, a suitable remedy will likely come immediately to mind. And while the remedy may be costly, or time consuming, or humbling, the price is cheap compared to the damage of living within a self-serving lie.

Regardless of whether the mending process yields a complete fix, the humility and goodwill exhibited as you work sincerely to fix what you have broken signals to others that while you are flawed, you can be trusted to be accountable.

Just as importantly, it signals to yourself that despite your flaws you are a person of integrity who is a builder, not a destroyer, and discover that you can also be trusted to fix yourself.

(Based upon wise insights of *Jordon Peterson*)

> "Opinions can be picked up cheap in the marketplace while such commodities as courage and fortitude and faith are in alarmingly short supply."
>
> Edward R. Murrow

Letting Fly

In an age when it seems that everyone is compelled to both express their opinion and to seek approval for having done so, it is easy to forget that your value is determined not by what you say, but by what you do.

Though opinions have always been a cheap commodity, today the gassy expression of certain views does earn a kind of social currency. That is: if your expressed opinion presses the right social buttons you will be paid the transient coin of acceptance by a certain crowd. That payment prompts many to frantically try to press that button again and again, desperate to get another dime's worth of social credit.

Of course, one can't trade social currency for food or merchandise. The coin of the social acceptance realm works like the points earned playing a video game- exchangeable only for right to play the game again. But this game never ends and never has a winner. Meanwhile, the fungible kind of currency that can be exchanged for necessities and luxuries comes not from letting opinions fly, but from creating real, tangible value for others. That is the stuff that others care about more than your opinion. Which is why they are willing to pay for what you do but are only willing to deposit some airy social currency for what you say.

Building the tangible value that others will pay for takes effort, and the greater the value the greater the effort required. In turn, increasing effort leaves decreasing time for the puffing out of opinions. Just so, there is usually an inverse relationship between the expression of opinions and the creation of value. One who outputs more viewpoints

OWN YOUR OUTCOMES
Self-responsibility VS The victim mindset

than results is merely vying for attention, ironically often by complaining about how poor the tangible results in their life have been.

So, while we all have the right to our opinions, supply far exceeds demand. By contrast, the creation of tangible value is always in demand, but it requires the individual to first build what is to be sold through time-consuming skill development, disciplined conscientiousness, and hard work. No wonder there are so many players pushing their keyboard levers to puff cost-free opinions into the digital atmosphere hoping to collect enough social coin to think of themselves as rich in some way. It just doesn't spend very well.

The tangible coin of tangible value does. But more than that, the value you create by what you do also accrues within yourself, compounding to enable even greater value creation in the future. That kind of value grows ever more concrete and substantial over time and lingers long after the air clears of all the opinions that have been let fly.

> *"Every time you tear a leaf off a calendar, you present a new place for new ideas and progress."*
>
> Charles Kettering

No Past Future

Load yourself into a time-travel vessel that looks like a DeLorean automobile, a homely phone booth, or perhaps a spectacular star ship and you're off to the past. In fiction, the trip backwards in time always seems intent on righting some error made in time-gone-by so that a different future can result in the present- the magical thinking of the forlorn. Putting aside the dubious wisdom of placing all bets on the notion that some specific, alternate sequence of cause-and-events can be made to unfold without unforeseen consequences, the notion lives only in the imagination anyway. You can learn from the past, but you can't tidy it up.

Even so, people do tend to waste a lot of emotional energy on imagining how they might right history for themselves. Perhaps such fantasies grow from our consumption of so many sci-fi stories that have cheery endings. Or worse, perhaps it is self-delusion into belief that what happened didn't really happen at all, and that current reality is merely a bizarre, unexplained non-sequitur. Such thoughts are not foreign to any of us. We'd all like to right history in some way.

But history is history and you can't undo it, though you can learn from past mistakes to do better in the future. Did poorly on that interview and missed the job opportunity? There is no point returning to the interviewer to reprise and improve your performance. The job has already been filled. Likewise, fantasizing about how extraordinarily well the interview went won't change a thing other than to make you feel ill-treated by the interviewer when you don't get the job. But if, instead, you take a lesson from the mistakes made during the interview you can tackle the next one with improved preparation and style.

 OWN YOUR OUTCOMES
Self-responsibility VS The victim mindset

Science-fiction stories notwithstanding, you can't go back to the future. Our attempts to right history or to remake it in our mind are just vanity acting out. Only by taking real ownership of what happened can you see what you might have done differently to change the outcome. Then, you can let go the past and move on to what's next better prepared.

There is simply no future in the past, but what you truthfully learn from it can shape a better future.

> *"He who fights, can lose. He who doesn't fight, has already lost."*
>
> Bertolt Brecht

No Biting

If you can't bite, or can't bring yourself to do so, you will probably be bitten.

Of course, you don't always have to bite. Flight is the other alternative and that just might be the best bet when faced with sudden, violent danger for which you are unprepared. Hysterical screaming might also be in order.

But regarding more common threats, the very act of fleeing or of ceding your territory only serves to encourage the current or a future attack. Aggressors opportunistically choose soft targets against which they can gain what they want with little risk while scrupulously avoiding targets that seem to pose real, return danger.

When animals clash over territory or food many first bare their teeth to demonstrate their ferocity, communicating their ability to inflict damage on the other. This is often sufficient to halt an attack before it starts. Aggressors may be dumb, but they are not stupid.

Among humans, discussion aimed at defusing the situation is the more civilized and desirable approach. But even in the best of circumstances this often doesn't work, and in some cases the illusion of dialog is used only to stall while secretly sharpening claws. Worse yet, when policies of appeasement are offered to the aggressor, that appeasement signals an inability or unwillingness to stand firm and bite back. Such toothlessness only encourages the aggressor in its aims, even spurring it to expand its malevolent goals.

There simply is no peace to be gained through weakness. Weakness is precisely what aggressors seek and seeing it inspires them to attack with even greater fervor.

To own a better outcome, you must be able and ready to bite when the time comes… so you don't have to.

> *"Patience is a great virtue... if you have time for that sort of thing."*

When Would Now be a Good Time?

We dream of the perfect moment when all the pieces seem to come together in our favor, allowing us to reach a superlative achievement. We celebrate and idolize perfect moments most plainly on display in sports competitions: the fighter who scores a 10th round knock-out after a grueling battle, the racer who makes an opportunistic pass on the final lap of the race, the Hail Mary pass for a touchdown that wins the game. The satisfaction of such moments is so thrilling and sublime that we wait with anxious anticipation for our own perfect moment to arrive, believing that it will be worth the delay.

Yet, for most of us the perfect moment will never come because perfect moments only look perfect in retrospect. In the present, a normal parade of moments includes some poor ones, many average ones, and a few good ones. We avoid the poor moments and usually ignore the average ones. But we also often shun good moments, waiting instead for that perfect moment to arrive. So, we wait moment after moment, not realizing that perfect moments are not delivered, they are made.

Good moments can be rendered perfect through concerted action. Consider the good job opportunity into which you invest your finest efforts then achieve remarkable success, the good chance to introduce yourself to a special someone which then evolves into the perfect relationship, the good trip to a good place that yields the adventure of a lifetime. Perfect moments live in disguise and only our action can reveal their true potential. What's more, we never know whether the good moment we come upon might be the only one we'll ever get.

So, grab hold of the lowly good moment now, because now isn't just a good time- it's the only time. Treat the good opportunity that comes along like the last you'll ever receive, and you can transform that good chance into the perfection you've been waiting for. It's time to stop waiting for the perfect moment that never comes.

When would NOW be a good time?

> *"We must use time as a tool, not as a couch."*
>
> John F. Kennedy

24

Every day we all face the same question whether or not we actually ask it of ourselves: How will I use these 24 hours to become the person I want to be and to reach my goals?

"No, no, no" you may say. *"I just want a day off!"*

Fair enough. But realize that those 24 hours are all that any of us have. Each day offers a perfectly equal allotment of the most precious resource we have- time. No one gets a second more or a second less. Sure, some days feel much longer than 24 hours, and some feel much, much shorter- particularly those days off. But know that, however long or short a day feels, once gone, those 24 hours are lost forever.

The long and short of the matter is that whatever your current obligations and activities may be, you allocate each block of 24 hours according to your priorities. You may think: *"I want to do this other thing, but I just don't have the time!"* Yet, the fact is that you have all the time there is. Which begs the question: are you prioritizing your use of time on the things that will take you to where you want to go or wasting it by traveling to frivolous dead ends.

For example, what if you cut back on your consumption of passive entertainment each day and spent that time learning something new instead. Even a small change in how you use those 24 hours can make a huge difference over the course of a year. Setting aside just 10 minutes a day to work on learning that something gives you a total of 60 hours of learning over the course of a year. What might be the valuable result of those 60 "extra" hours of learning? What might you then be able to do? Might you be closer to the person you want to be?

 *OWN YOUR OUTCOMES*
Self-responsibility VS The victim mindset

Not having the time cannot be the excuse for not moving toward your goals. Achievers don't have a time advantage. They are exactly as handicapped by time as are the rest of us. The difference is priorities. How could you reprioritize your use of time to move further in the right direction?

Time is the most valuable commodity that exists, and today, like every other day, you have all there is.

LANDING

Own Your Outcomes
Self-responsibility vs The victim mindset

Waiting for the world to make things right for you is a fool's game.

It can't.

The only practical response to a largely indifferent world is to take ownership of both the circumstances that were not of your making and of the outcomes that could be. Anything less is to be a mere passenger in a life that you should be driving- toward the better things that you envision.

Find yourself in a strange place where everything seems topsy-turvy and where the only way out is to undertake a hazardous journey through unknown lands? Isn't that pretty much what we all face? Then take a lesson from Dorothy who owned both her circumstances and the difficult effort needed to reach the outcome she sought. (Replace Kansas with your own goal here.)

Consider your own experience. When you have waited for things to happen by themselves, how often have you been disappointed? But when you have taken responsibility and action instead, how often have you felt empowered and found the way to better things despite the challenges?

You don't control the circumstances of your life, but you are entirely in control of how you respond to them. The journey to better things starts only when you take the wheel of your own life, proactively striving to make use of circumstances rather than being controlled by them.

Don't settle for victim status by making yourself a mere passenger in your own life. Be responsible for yourself and for the destination you seek. Take the wheel and drive.

> "Those who look into practical life will find that fortune is usually on the side of the industrious, as the winds and waves are on the side of the best navigators."
>
> *Samuel Smiles*

WHEN MONKEYS FLY

Be Skeptical
Questioning VS Doting acceptance of authority

Dorothy so believed in the power of the Wizard that she was willing to risk her life retrieving the Witch's broomstick on his promise to fulfil the travelers' wishes. Yet those promises turned out to be as empty as they were pretty, and the Wizard himself proved to be nothing but a mask of pomp and bluster veiling inadequacy.

It was a lesson hard learned by the girl, and one that often must be learned on our side of the rainbow too. Our leaders and the promises they make from behind the curtain of the political machine also often lack substance and are veiled by a mask pomp and bluster. Shame on them for their deceptions, but in the end, it is our own adoring embrace of pretty platitudes that renders the would-be wizards so toxic and dangerous.

The opposite approach, skepticism, is the impulse to pull aside the curtain to assess the veracity of claims and claimants; to question,

WHEN MONKEYS FLY

examine, and test both people and ideas. In stark contrast to the disappointment that often follows doting acceptance of authority, skepticism lets us find the truth.

In this flight we examine the anticritical impulses to embrace emotion-driven causes, to devotedly follow good intentions right into the abyss, to seek injurious redress for dubious injuries, and to argue only to win rather than to discover truth. In short, the folly that follows unskeptical behavior.

After all, if it sounds too good to be true, it is.

BE SKEPTICAL
Questioning VS Doting acceptance of authority

> "Hell isn't merely paved with good intentions; it's walled and roofed with them. Yes, and furnished too."
>
> Aldous Huxley

Drunk at the Wheel

Some societal programs possess so much emotional appeal that they persist long past the arrival of evidence that the road taken is not reaching the intended destination. Sometimes the nobility of a program's intentions has such intoxicating appeal that we simply drive on and on in a self-satisfied stupor, like the drunk who misses the "bridge out" sign and ends up floating down the river.

Witness the 1964 "War on Poverty", a government initiative intended to decrease the percentage of the US population living at the poverty level, which was 17.8% when the program began. This was a noble goal that spawned dozens of means-tested programs nationwide over the following 50 years, spending over $20 trillion in taxpayer dollars to reduce poverty. The result of that 50-year drive was a poverty rate of 14.8%, a drop of merely 3 percentage points. To put this meager improvement into context, consider that the 1950 poverty rate of 32% had already dropped by nearly half during the 14 years just prior to the start of the War on Poverty. Once the WOP programs were instituted, the decline in poverty virtually stopped.

This begs the question: Might the $20 trillion and a half century of effort have been put to more productive purposes? If previously rapid progress came to a near standstill after the program was put into place, might that be because the program's actions were actually counterproductive- driving in the wrong direction? Was it merely that we were so drunk on the elixir of our good intentions that for 50 years we missed the warning signs along the road?

Good intentions do not necessarily spawn good policy. Yet, in our self-righteous stupor we often imagine that our noble, good intentions alone will keep us headed in the right direction. So, we dismiss the caution flags along the road and ignore the alternative routes that we pass. The road trip that starts with the intoxicating mission to "do something important" can easily take the route of most drunken road trips, proceeding as a self-indulgent bacchanal that ends with debt and remorse, far from the destination you'd intended.

This inclination to hang on to unproven notions is known as "belief perseverance", a psychological phenomenon in which one persists in a belief despite evidence that contradicts it, unwilling to admit that the initial premise may no longer be true, or never had been. We're all susceptible to belief perseverance and to the companion mind trick of confirmation bias- the tendency to interpret all evidence as confirmation of one's existing beliefs or theories. Between the action of these two phenomena we're prone to confidently head down a lot of dead-end roads while refusing to turn back.

Consider another long-standing case of socio-political belief perseverance- the impassioned reaction generated by Paul Ehrlich's 1968 book: *The Population Bomb* and his later prediction that population increases would lead to the starvation deaths of about 4 billion people in the decade of the 1980s. In fact, the population did nearly double over the subsequent five decades, but food production increased far more than did population, diminishing food scarcity to its lowest level in history despite the population change. Yet many, including Ehrlich himself, still adhere to the notion that population driven mass starvation lies just over the horizon. That's 50 years of evidence that has failed to rouse the drunken minds of those who fell under the influence of belief perseverance.

Belief perseverance can also be motivated by nefarious goals. Consider the 17th century concept of the tabula rasa- the notion that the human mind is a blank slate without built-in content and upon which anything

BE SKEPTICAL
Questioning VS Doting acceptance of authority

may be written. This conception of the human mind has long been debunked. In his book, *The Blank Slate,* Steven Pinker elegantly illuminates how science has shown that, in contrast to this notion, the individual is not primarily shaped by culture and society but is instead significantly formed through evolutionary psychological adaptations. Genetically transmitted traits are central to the disposition of each human mind including intelligence, abilities, personality, instincts and other attributes. Yet the blank slate conception is jealously guarded even today, particularly by would be social engineers who desperately want to believe that they can write new instincts onto the minds of others, changing behaviors to comply with their own conceptions of how people should think and act. For such utopians drunk on the notion that they have everything figured out, genetic traits and dispositions represent an obstacle that must be rejected. Their beliefs persist despite all evidence to the contrary because their aspirations will be foiled otherwise.

Of course, it is not just dogmatic zealots who imbibe in this way. We all have a tendency to drunkenly believe in causes that we hold dear despite a lack of supporting data for our belief. Think of any notion in the current swath of causes that garner strong support despite weak evidence. Such beliefs are easily spawned in us, sometimes growing merely from misstated or out-of-context statistics that nevertheless give birth to ill-conceived but intoxicating causes. Like the travelers on a drunken road trip, devotees of the cause insist that they are "perfectly fine to drive" while being blind drunk to the signs of coming fiasco further down the road. They're just feeling so good about the trip.

If a friend exhibits signs of uncritical fealty to some lofty societal intention, metaphorically grab his/her car keys by challenging their feel-good notions with skeptical questions.

WHEN MONKEYS FLY

Friends don't let friends drive while under the intoxicating influence of good intentions.

BE SKEPTICAL
Questioning VS Doting acceptance of authority

"View Certainty with Skepticism"

The Rule of Exceptions

We humans seem wired to focus disproportionately upon people or groups who don't fit the norm. Call them the "exceptions." Such people stand out because they represent a minority of type or possess other untypical attributes. These exceptions may be individuals or groups who stand out because they achieve at an extreme level, or groups who seem always to lag behind all others, and yet other groups who simply stand out because they represent an exception to normal traits or behaviors.

We focus on the exceptional achievers for obvious reasons- their contributions are valuable, they represent our highest aspirations, and give us hope that we too can achieve. By contrast, the underachieving groups receive special attention and support because we hope that such can help them rise. But the ill-fitting groups seem to gain special attention not because they have positive or negative traits, but merely because they are exceptionally unusual.

Exceptional groups receive a disproportionate share of our limited time, attention, publicity, advocacy, legislative action, money, and other resources. While the achiever groups earn their attention and rewards, the underachieving groups receive it as a form of charity, while the merely unusual receive it because they tend to make a lot of noise about their unusual differences. Meanwhile, the "normies" who are not exceptional get less.

This disproportionate distribution creates a perverse incentive for the advocates of underachieving groups and for the merely unusual. The advocate knows that if their group can be made to appear greater in number, even more resources will flow to them. Then too is our natural tendency to overestimate the size of groups that are not in the main.

A 2022 study by YouGovAmerica found wide disparities between perceived and actual group sizes. For example: Americans perceived that 20% of the US population was Native American while the actual number is less than 1%; the Asian population was perceived to be 24%- reality 6%; the Black population was perceived to be 40%- reality 12.5%; the Gay or Lesbian population was perceived to be 24%- reality 3% plus 4% bisexual (though these numbers vary widely by age range); the Vegan/ Vegetarian population was perceived to be 25%- reality 5%; the Left-handed population was perceived to be 31%- reality 11%; just to site a few exceptional misperceptions.

These perceptions may be due to the high level of media attention given to groups that are not in the main. Groups are made to appear larger than they are when they show up frequently in the news, advertisements, and entertainment programming. They also seem to grow in size or stature when narratives about such groups are constructed to evoke sympathy or admiration above that of other groups. These perceptual levers are frequently used by advocates to manipulate opinion in favor of certain groups with the intent of securing exceptional attention, treatment, and resources for the group. Such manipulation may be well intended, may simply be greedy, or may serve a narcissistic need to feel virtuous. Sometimes, it's a bit each.

But the unavoidable result of such misrepresentation is a misallocation of our limited attention, time, and resources. And this price is paid predominantly by the normies who don't fit under any exception label and so get a lesser share of attention, time, and resources. In fact, it is usually the normies' resources, freedoms, and opportunities that are diminished, taken, or abolished to disproportionately benefit the exceptions instead. Adding insult to injury, these same people are also moralistically scolded not to complain about the burdens being imposed upon them and are threatened with chastisement, cancellation, or a

bigot label if they do. That's a lot of expense and ire to heap upon people who are merely asking that their own resources be allocated proportionately based upon facts rather than overwrought perceptions.

While we certainly don't want to forsake those human beings who aren't in the main, it is a very grave matter to disproportionately impose upon those who are. After all, those are people who have their own, albeit unexceptional, difficulties to deal with too, not to mention a wide range of quite exceptional difficulties that don't show on the surface and are not advertised.

Exceptions must be recognized as the exceptions they are and not allowed to rule simply because they have been exceptionally promoted. To maintain a fair system we must consider the exceptions with exceptional care.

On the Other Hand
Consider that:

- There are 136,000 accidental deaths per year in the US.
- 11% of the population is left-handed.
- Statistically, left-handed people are 5 times more likely to die in accidents than are right-handers.

This indicates that roughly 50,000 lefties are dying accidentally each year in the US alone, plausibly due, in part, to the fact that a significant percentage of the objects we use daily are designed for right-handers, making it more difficult and, for some items, more hazardous for lefties to use them.

Modest Proposal: *To counter this obvious bias against left-handers we must allocate significant resources to right (or is that "left") this wrong.*

To do so we must impose a set of regulations that will require left-friendly design of all things and processes. This must be done irrespective of cost and of any attendant impact on right-handers. After all, these new edicts may be able to save some lefties from injury or death!

On one hand, this is the quite sympathetic impulse to spare select people from harm. On the other hand is the fact that we're talking about just 11% of the population. Moreover, handedness is just one example of how we are all differently enabled. Consider our greatly differing heights, frame sizes, levels of intellect, athletic ability, attractiveness, and other factors, including the fact that some of us are left-handed. Those differing characteristics may, at times, convey either advantage or disadvantage dependent upon context. To wit: it is an advantage to be small of frame if you wish to be a gymnast, but a great hazard if you wish to play football.

Given the natural unequal distribution of attributes, it is incumbent upon everyone to leverage their own strengths to best effect and to work on, or around, their weaknesses. *(Spoken like a true right-hander.)* Each of our journeys will necessarily be different as each adapts according to his/her unique qualities and background. If you burn easily, perhaps the beach is not the place to hang out. For those who don't burn, an edict that requires everyone to purchase SPF 70 sunblock is closer to vengeance than to a solution.

While even right-handers may acknowledge that feasible accommodations should be made for special groups, we simply don't live in a world of unlimited resources or time. So, we must choose wisely concerning the accommodations in which we invest. Wise choices require that we challenge the presumptions of any proposed policies, assuring that we consider both context and scale as well as the intentional and unintentional costs they may place upon others.

 *BE SKEPTICAL*
Questioning VS Doting acceptance of authority

Life simply doesn't deal each of us the same hand. Ultimately, we must each play the one we have been dealt- even if it is left-handed. *(These right-handers are snarky.)*

> *"How many people have to die before we finally do something about dropping pianos?"*
>
> Attributed to Norm Macdonald

Shepherds

Modest Proposal: *"Since a significant number of people are seriously bitten by dogs each year, it is only common sense to outlaw ownership of dogs. Of the 4.5 million annual dog bites in the US, 800,000 require medical attention, 12,000 necessitate hospitalization, and about 50 result in death- 2017 CDC reporting. If outlawing all breeds seems too high a price, perhaps we can start by simply outlawing the dogs that appear to be most dangerous... German Shepherds certainly fit the bill!"*

This, and many other virtuous sounding political proposals, are modest only in so much as they cover up facts that run contrary to their arguments. In the case of dogs, consider the fact that dog bites represent only a very small percentage of the range of all injuries suffered by people each year, and that the German Shepherd breed is responsible for only a tiny fraction of those bites.

Still, the anti-Shepherd zealots cry: *"Just think of what a dog like that could do! We need to do something about this dog bite problem. No one needs a dog like that!"*, while secretly thinking: *"I don't have a German Shepard, so it's no loss to me. They scare me."*

The fact that German Shepherds also protect people and may actually prevent human injury at rates many times that of their undesired bites is of no concern to the emotional, anti-Shepard zealot. "Ban them all!" they cry. Yet, with such a ban, the plentiful good once gained from this breed is lost- the German Shepard as protector, as companion, or as service dog for millions of people- with no resulting bites. (There are nearly 4M German Shepherds in the US.) Still, the fervent, hysterical cry echoes: "If we can save just one person from injury it will be worth it!"

Such histrionic filibuster is rampant in politics, aiming to circumvent the questioning and fact-checking of presumptions that should precede such conclusions: What is the real proportion of good verses bad? How pervasive is this relative to other dangers? What are the other causative factors involved and what might we do about them? Where might the proposed policy prescriptions ultimately lead- at what cost and to whom? Etc.

Emotionally charged declarations are not arguments. Add crying, protests, and disproportionate media coverage and you are sure to whip-up a hysterical mob who desperately want to placate their feelings at the expense of other people's rights and privileges. When causation and context are put aside, a fitful, emotional argument can be made for the banning of nearly anything, including dogs. From there, the irrationality snowballs.

"Now that we've outlawed German Shepherds we should also outlaw those other scary breeds, like Pit Bulls and Rottweilers. And don't forget that even little dogs can cause some pretty nasty injuries when they bite your hand or ankle, not to mention the serious damage even a small dog might inflict on a child! They've all got to go. And don't get me started on cats... those claws are vicious and lightning fast. It's just common sense that we'd all be safer in a world without pets."

> *"Better to be paralyzed from the neck down than the neck up."*
>
> Charles Krauthammer

Privileged to Build Here

There are many kinds of privilege distributed across the population that may be linked either to immutable characteristics or to circumstance. These include commonly cited kinds of privilege, but also benefits like beauty-based privilege, athleticism-based privilege, intellect-based privilege, and talent-based privileges for music, writing, singing, dancing, comedy, craftsmanship, problem-solving, tenacity, leadership, science, analytical thinking, design, entrepreneurship, communication… the list goes on and on. Just which of these privileges trump which others depends upon context and upon one's perspective. Then too, some people possess several such privileges simultaneously, for example: the person who is really smart, really attractive, and also really athletic. If we are honest we'd admit that we often secretly envy and hate such people, rather like high school wallflowers who sneer about the cheer leaders and jocks who are so damn popular. We dislike such disparities so much that any privileged attribute that we don't possess can stimulate schemes to eradicate that privilege to "level the playing field."

In the dystopian future world of Kurt Vonnegut's short story: *Harrison Bergeron*, society deals with such privileges by handicapping those who possess them, thus eliminating the advantages that those attributes would naturally confer to the holder. Those who are beautiful must wear masks to cloak their beauty, those who are strong are saddled with heavy weights to make them struggle, and those who are intelligent have their minds disrupted by radios installed to muddle their keen thinking.

Note that the effort is not to aid those who are less athletic so they may further develop, nor to help those who are less beautiful to enhance their appearance, nor to educate those who are less smart so they may become more intellectually able. The impulse to "level the playing field" is not a drive to build up, but rather, to tear down. We can see this paralyzing impulse at work today in the lowering of academic standards, the celebration of the ugly as beautiful, and in the chastisement of those who excel. Despite proclamations about the need for such destruction in pursuit of "social justice", at base, the impulse to tear down is merely envy acting out.

Yet, in the context of history we are all privileged to be here, living in the most free and prosperous time ever. We all enjoy far more privilege today than our ancestors did just 100 years ago. But our relative prosperity was achieved only by overcoming the efforts of those whose envious impulse was to tear down. Our current privilege grew from the effort of talented people who relentlessly practiced the art of building-up instead. But that feat can continue only if we return to a system that does not paralyze high level abilities but rather, celebrates, rewards, and develops them.

Consider your own experience. When you have stooped to demean or hobble the advantageous attributes of another, how did it make you feel? Probably rather petty and mean. By contrast, when you have striven to improve another's weak point, how did you feel? Probably like a good person. Because you were.

Be skeptical of those who declare the need to tear down or disadvantage some to overcome "privilege". They are selling a dystopia in which the most able are oppressed yet none are raised up. Thus, we tear down our society person-by-person and group-by-group. By contrast, when great abilities are celebrated and encouraged to flourish, even those who have farther to travel gain new opportunities, are inspired to grow, and we build ever higher together.

Building expands the level of privilege available to all.

> *"A great deal of intelligence can be invested in ignorance when the need for illusion is deep."*
>
> Saul Bellow

Lawyer-up

"Lawyer-up" is the modern equivalent of the old-west phrase "saddle-up." Both are a call to action in preparation for a conflict that we aim to win in a do-or-die showdown. Like those steed-riding heroes of old, lawyers are trained and practice to win in favor of a particular outcome although, unlike the westerns of yesteryear, it is not always easy to tell the difference between the good guys and the bad guys.

That is not criticism. It simply expresses the nature of the job. The legal justice system works only if attorneys behave in just this way- arguing vigorously in favor of the position being taken by their side, regardless of who's good or bad. It is a showdown, and we need the attorneys fighting forcefully on both sides of the conflict. Yippee-ki-yay.

The parties to any legal showdown naturally leverage whatever information supports their position or which disparages the opposing position. For the attorney, arguing a case is an endeavor to win. If deeper insights don't support the position being argued, those insights are downplayed and argued against. The job is not to advocate on behalf of objective truth. The job is to win on behalf of a predetermined position. And again, this is not criticism. The attorney role functions as intended, and conformance with this operating principle is mandatory. The attorney who intentionally fails to argue the best case possible on behalf of their client can ultimately face disbarment.

But differentiate this approach from that used in proper business decision making. There, the success and survival of an organization depends upon finding the deepest truths possible about what works and what does not, both within the organization and in the marketplace. The organization must then act upon those deep truths to implement whatever changes must be made to assure its success. Differing viewpoints are discussed, but it is understood that simply winning an argument on behalf of a predetermined position does not create business success. Only acting on objective truths can. The business leader who fails to find those truths and to act upon them faces firing while the business itself faces bankruptcy. Pre-determined positions be damned.

Yet, in the law, the attorney who successfully argues in favor of a pre-determined position, regardless of any deeper truths, is celebrated. Truth be damned. This is the way the law is designed to work and, once again, that is no criticism. It is simply a recognition of the framework that attorneys are trained for and aligned to by the nature of the role.

But this difference between legal and business operating principles and effects is seen starkly in our political system which has become dominated by attorneys. In theory, making law should be more easily accomplished by those educated in law. However, in practice, the explicit training, routine, and perhaps the inherent mind-set of lawyers likely impedes the more business-like pursuit of underlying truths necessary to effective governance. The natural inclination of the attorney is to formulate a position then argue against all others. Yet, as in business, merely winning on behalf of a predetermined position won't produce a superior governmental product. At best, vigorous argument leads to compromises between the opposing positions.

But compromises don't unearth the deeper truths needed to solve problems. They are simply negotiated trade-offs between pre-determined positions and, thus, suffer from the Middle Ground fallacy. In the business world, a simple compromise between opposing internal positions won't satisfy the real-world needs of customers either. Only acting on objective truths can hope to do that. But in business, better do it quickly because dissatisfied customers will promptly vote with their feet, moving their patronage to the competitor that's doing a better job at addressing the objective truth of their needs. Meanwhile in government, years separate the chances that the dissatisfied citizenry have to express their discontent by voting. Between votes legislators congratulate themselves on what a fine job they did arguing their pre-determined positions. But opinion polls give an indication of just how the citizenry rates the "product" of the legislature. Within the US that rating consistently falls below the 1-star level. How many business organizations that consistently get 1-star ratings continue to exist?

There is a structural problem with the way we make law. Yet, again, it must be stated that lawyers fulfill a vital role within the legal justice system and are elegantly equipped for that challenge. The question here is whether our legislators should come to the table with the litigator's mindset and habits or with the businessperson's disposition instead.

Currently we watch a perpetual showdown in the halls of government driven by people who are disposed to argue on behalf of predetermined positions rather than to uncover deeper insights and ferret out solutions. Might it be wise to challenge the presumption that those with legal training make the best political leaders?

(PS- Please don't sue me over this viewpoint.)

BE SKEPTICAL
Questioning VS Doting acceptance of authority

> *"Be thankful for quality competitors who push you to your limit."*
>
> Michael Josephson

Runners

Olympic runners do not argue with each other about who is faster. They race to prove it.

Those who run businesses operate with a similar kind of direct competition. They hunt for opportunities to solve problems in new and practical ways, place real bets on their ideas by leveraging funds willingly contributed by themselves and by investors, and get immediate feedback from the market about the real-world value of their offerings as measured by customers' ongoing willingness to trade for those offerings. Ultimately, they live or die by their ability to learn from mistakes and to adapt, improving the value they provide to customers. To win, they must run a better race than their competitors.

By contrast, those who run government policy seem to be occupied primarily with argumentation concerning who is right. They largely respond to known problems by bickering over opinions, (and sometimes by promoting preposterous schemes), fund their initiatives using money taken from taxpayers, and lack a short-loop feedback and correction mechanism concerning the value of their efforts (i.e.: unlike customers, citizens can't refuse to pay for services they don't like and can only vote every few years). And because they live and die by vote, an enormous amount of time and energy is expended by politicians to convince constituents of their value, often by obscuring their mistakes and by making false promises.

Is that too bitter an assessment? Here's the point: Competition among runners or in any other domain tends to expose the truth with athletic agility. Posturing and promises don't. Look only at the track record.

> "If we do not openly discuss our moral differences, we are doomed to bloody battle over them."

Dead Certain

It can be reasonably asserted that certain crimes are so heinous that the death penalty is a suitable punishment. But while the punishment might fit the crime, there remains a question of principle concerning whether or not that punishment ought to be doled out. Consider this perspective:

While the guilt of a party, legally determined under fair and accepted process can reasonably be assumed, it cannot be trusted with absolute certainty. There is nearly always a chance of false conviction. Such false convictions have and do occur, sometimes even in cases where the accused has confessed to the crime. Fortunately, when a wrongful conviction is discovered, we attempt to right the miscarriage of justice by freeing the person and perhaps given recompence. But in the case of a death penalty that has been carried out, the wrongfully convicted cannot be freed. This penalty is irreversible.

Consider then the presumption that defends the death penalty, i.e.: that we have irrefutable evidence of guilt. Fair enough. Such instances exist. But if iron clad certainty is not possible in a case, wise skepticism would require that instead of meting out the execution penalty we dictate imprisonment instead to preserve the option for righting a mistaken conviction if later discovered.

The death penalty closes all possibilities. A healthy skepticism would keep some open.

LANDING

Be Skeptical
Questioning vs Doting acceptance of authority

"Laws are like sausages; it is better not to see them being made" (Otto von Bismarck). More than any other ingredient, presumptions are poured into the sausage grinder of public policy. The turning of the crank is too often powered by doting allegiance to questionable goals, uncommon exceptions, or outright phantoms. As such, this grinder often operates merely to pulverize evidence that contradicts the position taken.

Challenging presumptions requires pulling back the curtain of the political machine like the tugging insistence of a curious little dog. That happens by asking tough questions about policy presumptions and expecting real answers: What is the evidence for and the evidence to the contrary? How do we know? What are the benchmarks against which we should compare the proposal? What is the proportional scale of the issue? What motives are in play? What are the alternatives? What factual or logical flaws are being cloaked behind the claims? Just who is that man behind the curtain?

Consider your own experience. How often have you witnessed the enactment of policies based solely upon theories that were pursued with intense emotional fervor despite reasonable evidence to the contrary? Have you noticed positions and policies of this kind that are at work currently- perhaps even some of those that you'd like to believe in?

You can be sure that every turn of the crank will be preceded by the expression of good intentions. Ignore them to avoid the road to Hell that they pave. Instead, exercise the wise habit of challenging the presumptions of, and about, those who would turn it-

with the kind of skepticism born of the Kansas prairie.

BE SKEPTICAL
Questioning VS Doting acceptance of authority

> *"Science is the belief in the ignorance of experts."*
>
> Richard Feynman

WHEN MONKEYS FLY

Confront Fashionable Nonsense
Calling out the ridiculous VS Woke indoctrination

Upon her awakening return to Kansas, Dorothy vaguely realized that the beautiful Land of Oz was just a fanciful dream. Perhaps the dream's pretty impossibilities were spawned by the shock of having her dog taken away, her terror amidst the twister, and a subsequent bump on the head. Finding herself in a suddenly frightening place, Dorothy sought an alternate world of pretty imaginings to supplant the reality of that moment in her Kansas life.

Similarly, when we feel ill-used by established standards and norms it is only natural to make up some new ones. The question is: are we abandoning those standards and norms for the better, or because the old ones recognize difficult realities that we now prefer to ignore?

In this flight we look at the current impulse to tear down what was built up over centuries whenever a crack in its surface is found, and to subvert language in the service of the crack-finding ideology.

WHEN MONKEYS FLY

Knowing the difference between what is trending and what is true requires the wise habit of confronting nonsense, however fashionable it may be at the time.

> *"Everything in the world displeases me: but, above all, my displeasure in everything displeases me."*
>
> Friedrich Nietzsche

The Postmodern Abyss

Postmodern art is easy to pick out in the gallery. Just examine the faces of those looking upon a work. Some hold a rapturous gaze while others just stare quizzically. Contrast that to the mesmerized expressions displayed by everyone visiting the Renaissance collection. Perhaps it's just a matter of taste.

But Postmodern philosophy is another matter. David Horowitz has suggested that this philosophy stems from a well-meaning effort to abolish all things that are perceived to have caused brutal conflict in the 19th and 20th centuries. This interpretation of Postmodern logic might be expressed as follows: In the modern era countries fought over borders- so there must be no borders; religions fought over doctrine- so there must be no beliefs; people fought over material wealth- so there must be no incentive to become more prosperous; individuals felt burdened by standards of morality, beauty, and truth, so relativistic standards must replace them such that everyone can be "moral", "beautiful" and possess their own "truth"; and, most broadly, parties fought over ideas, so there must be no difference of opinion.

No boundaries, no beliefs, no individual prosperity, no standards, no debate. Postmodernism is, at its core, an attempt to eliminate all the aspects of life that make life worth fighting for. But this is also crucial stuff that makes life worth living.

Postmodernism is really just a fancy way of believing in nothing. This wispy brand of thinking often fuels those who promote the elimination of various freedoms, the destruction of the rule of law, the quashing of speech, the damning of beauty and truth, the denigration of exceptionalism, and the heralding of mediocrity.

Some gaze rapturously upon Postmodern philosophy, believing that its decrees will eliminate the conflicts that come with being human. But their gaze fails to perceive the inhuman and unlivable abyss behind the frame.

> *"Political language... is designed to make lies sound truthful... and to give an appearance of solidity to pure wind."*
>
> *George Orwell*

Newspeak 2

In his book *1984*, George Orwell envisioned a nightmarish world where "right" thinking was enforced, in part, through the imposition of a new lexicon of socio/political terminology called: "Newspeak". Currently, a new, newspeak seems to be taking shape under power of similar motives. This lexicon includes both novel terms that assert particular conclusions and the redefinition of long-used terms, each an apparent attempt to align thinking to certain synthetic notions of reality. These contemporary inventions tend to be deployed with an implicit assumption that the new and redefined terms somehow embody unassailable truths.

Unassailability is a standard that boarders on the divine, so a little clarity in definition and some critical deconstruction would seem prudent prior to the consecration of "Newspeak 2". What follows is an examination of some of the most popular Newspeak 2 terms:

Cultural Appropriation

"The act of taking or using things from a culture that is not your own, especially without showing that you understand or respect this culture"
Cambridge Dictionary

In popular use of the term, "cultural appropriation" implies an act of oppression that either knowingly or unknowingly steals identity and/or opportunity from people whose native origin is that of the culture being appropriated. Such appropriation consists primarily of adopting or adapting some part of a culture's traditions, dress, food, expressions, or other elements into an individual's or a people's own behavior or customs.

But adoption and adaptation are not usurpation. Such cultural elements can continue to be held by the originating culture even if other cultures adopt or adapt these into their separate cultures. Moreover, cultural elements of old are often morphed by the source culture itself into forms unrecognizable by its originators. Frequently this happens through its own process of adopting and adapting elements from other cultures. Cultures always evolve.

Adoption or adaptation of elements across cultures lets us embrace and build upon good things found elsewhere. It results in a richer, more varied, and more interesting experience of life because it enables cultures to grow as they see fit, both within and outside the originating cultures.

The anti-appropriation position seems to flow from a presumption that each identity group must never deign to grow beyond its native culture by adopting or adapting elements of others. This would be rather like establishing a rule that dog breeds must never be mixed to assure that each breed remains pure. But that is not how we got all those wonderful breeds in the first place, and it certainly precludes the creation of great new mutts in the future.

In any case, do Labradors or Poodles suffer any diminution of reputation because Labradoodles now exist?

Cultures procreate as they see fit and are forever evolving. Preventing such only appropriates a future of neutered stagnation.

Democratic Socialism

"Socialism, or a modified form of socialism, achieved by a gradual transition by and under democratic political processes." Dictionary.com

In popular application the term is often mistakenly used to describe any countries (e.g.: Denmark) which feature free market economies coupled to extensive tax-funded spending on social programs. But these examples have nothing whatsoever to do with socialism, democratic or otherwise. (Socialism is defined as: *"Any economic or political system based on government ownership and control of important businesses and methods of production"* Cambridge Dictionary).

In fact, free markets are antithetical to Socialism. The "democratic" modifier refers only to the political method by which socialism might be put into place- that is, by vote. So, while Denmark and other commonly cited examples do have democratic political systems, they feature free market economic systems, not socialist economic systems. The term: "Democratic Socialism" simply does not fit. Which is why such countries actively reject being referred to as examples of Democratic Socialism. Former Danish Prime Minister Lars Lokke Rasmussen has stated: *"I would like to make one thing clear. Denmark is far from a socialist planned economy. Denmark is a market economy."*

By contrast, perhaps the best recent example of actual Democratic Socialism would be Venezuela, where a leader was elected to power democratically and where, subsequently, Socialist economic policies were instituted by that leader (Hugo Chavez). Extensive, tax-funded spending on social programs, powered by the product of free markets (such as in Denmark), are a completely different organism.

Fair

"Treating someone in a way that is right or reasonable, or treating a group of people equally and not allowing personal opinions to influence your judgment" Cambridge Dictionary

In common parlance the term unfair is often misused as a label for any situation in which the outcomes of different people are unequal, that is, not equally distributed, regardless of individual merit or context. In Newspeak 2, fair no longer means fair- it means equal in outcome. Which itself can be quite unfair.

Inequality

"The quality of being unequal or uneven" Merriam-Webster Dictionary

The difficulty with this commonly used term is that it now frequently comes loaded with the presumption that bigotry must be the cause for whatever inequality is being described. Yet, human capabilities are never equally distributed across groups of people, so it is simply nonsensical to suggest that their outcomes must always be equal.

It's like asserting that the NBA is bigoted against short men because, otherwise, there would be an equal distribution of tall and short players. Yet, however skilled a man may be, at 5'-4", he simply cannot succeed in the NBA. He is just too short. The unequal distribution of tall and short men in the NBA is not an indication of bigotry against either short men in general nor against races that are characteristically shorter in statue than others. It is merely an indication of the crucial necessity for certain human attributes (in this case, tallness) to a particular role (here- basketball player). That attribute is unequally distributed among the population, with some groups exhibiting greater levels of tallness and other groups exhibiting lesser levels. So, some groups will seem to be underrepresented simply because a smaller percentage of group members currently possess the necessary attribute(s).

This is not to say that there can be no bigotry at play, of course. It is merely to point out that if we start with an assumption that bigotry is the precipitating cause of all disparities, we are primed for confirmation bias, forever finding evidence of our foregone conclusions while reflexively obfuscating evidence to the contrary. That is both a mistake and a lost opportunity because it might be possible to help groups change key attributes so they may better compete. While improving height might be out of the range of possibilities, most other attributes are not. But when we start with the assumption that bigotry is the reason for different outcomes, we don't even seek such solutions.

By definition, different groups of human beings have different attributes. Some attributes are superficial (e.g.: skin color), while others are functional (e.g.: tallness in the NBA). We don't want discrimination based upon superficial attributes (that's bigotry), but we absolutely must grade merit among functional attributes (that's meritocracy).

Yet, too often, claims of inequality are based only upon examination of superficial attributes without consideration of other, meritocratic factors.

Those short guys just can't dunk the ball.

[Fill-in-the-blank] Justice

"The quality of being fair and reasonable" Lexico

Myriad contractions that leverage the word "justice" exist, the most common being: "social justice." The term was first coined by Catholics in the early 19th century to encourage the habit of non-governmental association and cooperation that they believed was needed to cope with the transition to a post-agrarian world. However, current use of this term seems to stem largely from the contemporary misinterpretation of inequality (as described above). The implicit assumption in this use of the term is that: if all things are not equal among people, some social injustice must have been perpetrated.

Other contractions made with the word "justice" granularize this notion, attempting to lend moral authority and/or urgency to particular points of view. All express a presumed vision of rightness that often stems from the aforementioned misinterpretation of inequality. But adding the word "justice" to the moniker of such causes suggests a cynical attempt to circumvent critical assessment of its notions. Who doesn't want justice to prevail?

Yet, assessing the actual merit of this or that "justice" necessitates the frank answering of a couple questions: How are you measuring the injustice against which you are campaigning and what data proves that it is the result of injustice rather than some other source? A simple statistical inequality between groups does not explain why the inequality exists.

Seeking redress of actual injustices is a noble cause. But the uncritical garnishment of any cause with the term "justice" only serves to diminish whatever real merits the cause may have. We all want justice. But the case for change must be made with reason, evidence, and debate so that others hear more than just the primal emotion of blanket proclamations about (fill-in-the-blank) justice.

Mansplaining

"The act of explaining something to someone in a way that suggests that they are stupid; used especially when a man explains something to a woman that she already understands" Cambridge Dictionary

The dilemma in this term's use is that it assumes that the listener can be certain of the intent of the speaker and can also be certain that the speaker is aware that the listener already knows the information being conveyed. That's a lot of assumptions and interpretation. It is also suspect that the term is: "mansplaining"- making it a derisive term aimed only at men. But do not women also stoop to condescension? The lady doth protest too much, methinks. (Was that mansplaining?)

Microaggression

"A subtle but offensive comment or action directed at a minority or other nondominant group that is often unintentional or unconsciously reinforces a stereotype." Dictionary.com

Here the dilemma is that by inventing a formal term to describe miniscule offences that are likely unintentional, we artificially elevate their importance well beyond their microscopic reality. It also tends to pour cold water on interactions between people as each party haltingly struggles to analyze the potential micro-impact of their every word, phrase, or gesture.

Mature people scarcely even notice such microaggressions, and it's not for lack of reading glasses. Their personal offence radar simply isn't that sensitive, perhaps because they are less self-focused or perhaps possess a broader perspective on the attributes of actual aggressions like a criminal accusation or a punch in the face. Such individuals, thus, put microaggressions in their place as the evanescent phantoms that they are.

No one benefits from being so paranoid and so brittle that they can be hurt by microaggressions. The reality is that some people will intentionally make vaguely unpleasant remarks (shame on them), some will do so accidentally (oops), and some will make such remarks believing that they were saying something nice (nice try). Mature people understand that we are all quite imperfect in the ways we communicate and interact, and that such micro-events should simply be dismissed as the miniscule scrapes they are.

If a really, tiny scrape deeply injures you, it is your own internalized perception of the scrape that is doing the damage. In reality, you don't even need a band-aid.

[Fill-in-the-blank] Phobic

"Having a strong dislike of something." Cambridge Dictionary

Contractions using the word "phobic" are abundant. In the socio-political context, such expressions are too often deployed simply as a bludgeon. The wielder of this bludgeon disingenuously smashes it against the character of those who he/she wants to stop from expressing facts, observations, or opinions which oppose the views of the wielder. Bludgeoning the speaker with a [*fill-in-the-blank*] phobic term is intended to discredit that person as a bigot, irrespective of their statement's merit or lack thereof. The bludgeon is most often deployed against arguments that the wielder cannot refute. Much easier to simply place an offensive label on a foe than to come up with a meaningful argument. *"If you cannot prove a man wrong, don't panic. You can always call him names."* (Oscar Wilde)

Of course, there are people who can rightly be called phobic due to their attitudes towards one or another group. But this derisive expression is both overused and frequently misapplied. So much so, in fact, that should you find yourself being called a [*fill-in-the-blank*] phobic, you can likely assume that the name caller has no meaningful evidence to refute your position and is simply swinging the verbal bludgeon caveman style instead.

[Fill-in-the-blank] Privilege

"A right, immunity, or benefit enjoyed only by a person beyond the advantages of most." Dictionary.com

But in its more contemporary use: *"The belief that members of particular groups, sexualities, genders, sexes, race, etc. are afforded advantages in society for being a member of said group."* Urban Dictionary

The issue with this term is that it depends upon a preposterously oversimplified view of human beings. Declaring that someone possesses privilege by virtue of their demographic characteristics is to ignore that the circumstances of our individual lives are enormously complex, involving millions of factors and interrelationships, and that these factors are in constant change. Boiling all that down to a simplistic label that points to a few simple attributes sets aside this complexity and serves to dehumanize us all, not to mention unjustifiably vilifying or disempowering some.

Consider this scenario: One young person is of sub-average intelligence, grew up in the foster care system, never finished high school, and exhibits both a stutter and odd facial tics. A second young person possesses superior intellect, grew up in an affluent, intact family, attended an Ivy League college and is well spoken and attractive. How much privilege is possessed by each? Can that privilege or lack thereof be boiled down to a single demographic characteristic?

What if the demographics you first imagined for these two people were flipped between them? Still think it is a singular demographic attribute that produces privilege?

Now add a few more circumstances to the story of the second young person- the one who seems privileged: Turns out that they were abused throughout their entire childhood but never revealed this to anyone. This person also had to fight a childhood disease which left them frail and, worse, they have recently been diagnosed with a late-stage recurrence of the disease that will almost certainly end their young life. Now who is the more privileged young person?

The real-world complexities that exist in every human life make the victim/privilege status gambit a shallow, political ploy that consciously glosses over the deeper human issues involved. Does it make sense to shame, silence or punish either person in the above, simple example for demographic attributes and conditions they had nothing to do with, while ignoring all their other attributes and conditions?

"Yes- if all other things are equal", one might respond. But all other things are never equal, because "all other things" includes millions of factors.

And that is what makes the privilege gambit a fool's game.

Intersectionality

"The theory that the overlap of various social identities, as race, gender, sexuality, and class, contributes to the specific type of systemic oppression and discrimination experienced by an individual" Dictionary.com

Intersectionality theory is a fellow to the notions about privilege. The theory presumes that a kind of point-score can be assigned to people based upon the particular combination of privilege or disadvantages that they possess, with multiple disadvantages effectively adding to their score. It essentially offers a kind of handicapping system.

This loose theory possesses superficial merits, however, in popular application it is often exalted as the final solution to disparities of outcome by whatever group wields its power. But its practical deficiency is revealed by the simplistic assumptions about privilege it depends upon, as described in the prior essay.

Moreover, given that human beings are characterized by millions of factors and circumstances, just who decides which ones should be components of the rubric, which should not, and what value is assigned to each? Perhaps even more important is the question: What do we do with this rubric? Do we actively diminish the opportunities of less disadvantaged people- institutionalizing relative discrimination against certain categories of people based upon the assumptions of the rubric?

Should we not, instead, assess each human being in the fuller context of their life, on their demonstrated merits, and according to their actual behavior? Dr. King profoundly envisioned a world in which we are each judged not on the color of our skin, but on the content of our character. What of that profound aspiration?

Safe Space

Safe: *"Not in danger or likely to be harmed."* Cambridge Dictionary

The term "safe" has been concatenated to form multiple extensions such as "safe person" and "safe environment", though "safe space" is the head of the family. Safety is generally a pretty good thing, so the difficulty with such terms has to do with the nature of the threats from which the "safe" option is offering protection. In the current parlance, the threat is often as trivial as the hearing of differing points of view with which the safety-seeker disagrees, or which makes him/her feel uncomfortable.

Of course, seeking safety from the expression of such points of view is antithetical to the free exchange of ideas- the very thing that allows us all to learn from or, at least, to better understand each other. Rushing off to a safe space when alternate views are presented is the equivalent of the toddler who sticks his fingers in his ears when being told to go to bed, simultaneously shouting: *"I can't hear what you're saying! I don't have to!"*

It should make us all feel uncomfortable when someone refuses to hear an opposing point. We should all be willing need to hear each other, especially when we disagree. It is through our discussion of disagreements that we learn and gain insight. It is also one of the key reasons that we are all needed- i.e.: our diversity of perspectives and ideas.

"Safe spaces" shut down this essential tool of understanding by effectively operating as helplessness indoctrination zones, places where overly delicate minds are conditioned to become even more fragile and isolated.

Trigger

"Something that causes someone to feel upset and frightened because they are made to remember something bad that has happened in the past." Cambridge Dictionary

"Trigger" is commonly used in such expressions as: "trigger warning" or "I'm triggered." The term itself was borrowed from the psychological lexicon where it was originally used to describe stimuli that spur a powerful emotional reaction related to serious trauma previously experienced by the sufferer, such as the Post-traumatic Stress sometimes experienced by battlefield soldiers. But colloquial use of the term has diluted its meaning to include upset resulting from reminders of any number of minor experiences, and even to the hearing of ideas that the hearer presently finds distasteful.

The trigger warning declaration is a caution that something is about to happen that might possibly trigger an emotional response in somebody. (Is there anything that doesn't fit that description?) It offers one the opportunity to avoid, rather than to confront the matter. Serious issues notwithstanding, this well-meaning attempt at protection against all manner of potential upset tends to leave the very people whose emotions are being protected emotionally stuck in place.

All of this is quite a shame because there are people who have had objectively traumatic experiences, and we should be cautious not to stimulate memories of those. However, diluting the term to the point that it can refer to virtually any trivial experience that caused someone stress of some kind, or to virtually any topic or speaker with whom you might believe you have strong disagreement, does a disservice to those who have suffered real trauma. What's more, overcoming your discomfort with non-devastating memories is often supported by confronting those memories, whereas avoiding them tends only to preserve their triggering power.

Trigger warning: Don't run away if you hear a trigger warning.

The [Fill-in-the-blank] Word

"A polite way of referring to [a] very offensive word." Cambridge Dictionary

Substitute the first letter of any forbidden word in the blank here. The forbidden words are forbidden because when used today as a slur they are especially hurtful or vulgar. Fair enough. Courtesy and decency should dictate that they not be used in such a fashion.

WHEN MONKEYS FLY

However, there is a key difference between the use of such words as a contemporary slur and when simply found in prose representing the colloquial language of an era or a character. Context is everything. Erasing such uses from works of prose changes the meaning or effect of the writing. The writer had likely used the word intentionally to convey a certain context, create an effect, deliver a certain meaning, or perhaps their work was simply written during an era when different norms in the use of language prevailed. Such prose can only be properly understood by retaining its full use of language however offensive that language might now be. Comprehension requires acknowledgement of context.

In any case, words have no power except the power we assign to them. Valdemort will not suddenly appear if you read the name from the book's page aloud rather than substituting: "The V word."

CONFRONT FASHIONABLE NONSENSE
Calling out the ridiculous VS Woke indoctrination

> "When the debate is lost, slander becomes the tool of the loser."
>
> Attributed to Socrates

Self-immolation

If Homer Simpson haphazardly sets himself on fire, it's hilarious. He might frantically dance around the room shouting: "Ouch, ouch, ouch, ooooh, yikes, ouch, ouch, oooooouch!" and so on in typical Homer style. Of course, Homer is a cartoon character and will be back in full health for the next episode. It's easy to laugh at animated self-immolation.

But reputational immolation lacks such cartoon humor. Its fires are sparked by the insistence that all the behavior, words, representations, and works of people, living and dead, must comport with contemporary knowledge and perspectives. If they do not, the impulse is to burn down the reputation and artifacts of that person. No allowance is made for the historical context in which the person lived, nor for their profound accomplishments made within that context. All are judged only by contemporary norms and assumptions, prompting some to call for the burning down of all things associated with the assailed person including books, movies, statues, and even names. C.S. Lewis called this impulse "Chronological Snobbery" which he described as: "The uncritical acceptance of the intellectual climate common to our own age and the assumption that whatever has gone out of date is on that account discredited."

In our present, foolish world this immolation is purported to protect contemporary people from past attitudes or behaviors by vilifying, then erasing those who lived according to the standards of different eras. Such "canceling" of historical figures is a form of burning people at the stake for the crime of having lived within the context of their own time rather than ours. Should the present virulence of this destructive impulse continue, virtually all historical figures will be burned in time because no past life can escape the shallow judgement of those without historical perspective.

Those who promote vilifying historical figures and works would be wise to consider how they are propping open the door for the future vilification of their own lifetime accomplishments- at a not-so-distant time when societal norms differ from those accepted today. They are building the pyre that also burn their own reputation at the stake in time.

Their shortsightedness is a form of self-immolation. Ouch.

LANDING

Confront Fashionable Nonsense
Calling out the ridiculous vs Woke indoctrination

The Inquisitor in George Orwell's book *1984* tortured the protagonist, Winston, into agreement with a patent falsehood. The Inquisitor held up 4 fingers, declared that he was showing 5 fingers instead, then tortured Winston until he agreed.

Acquiescence to the idea that words mean things that they never have, that history can be taken out of context, and that time-tested principles must be abolished is to stare into the bright lights of the Inquisitor and declare: "I see 5".

Like the crystal ball used by the Wicked Witch of the West to coerce Dorothy, propogandists paint word pictures of a world that does not exist so they may gain control of us.

Confront the sophistry that so often propels popular culture. Even passive acceptance of nonsensical arguments is an abdication of both your essential integrity and, ultimately, your very soul.

WHEN MONKEYS FLY

> *"Rage and frenzy will pull down more in half an hour than prudence, deliberation, and foresight can build up in a hundred years."*
>
> Edmund Burke

CONFRONT FASHIONABLE NONSENSE
Calling out the ridiculous VS Woke indoctrination

WHEN MONKEYS FLY

Put Away Childish Things
Shedding naive notions VS Chronic gullibility

Dorothy's difficult journey in the Land of Oz unwrapped her from the safe protection of her Kansas home. While the land was beautiful, it was full of dangers that upset her naïve view as she learned of the wickedness and disappointments of that world. Indeed, whenever we remove the bubble-wrap of naïve notions we become subject to injury, at least of the emotional kind.

In this flight we examine how protection of the young from the emotional bumps and bruises of life's road has become an obsession of parents and educators and has been embraced by young people themselves- a habit that can only lead to the forestalling of adulthood.

The unwrapping of naïve conceptions is a necessary part of each young person's journey toward maturity. It is only through direct contact with harsh realities that young people can acquire the opposite of protected naivete: Wisdom.

The bubble wrap must go.

> *"Maturity is reached the day we don't need to be lied to about anything."*
>
> Frank Yerby

Of Copernicus and Youth

In childhood the world seems to orbit around you. The adults in a child's life focus their time, energy, money, and attention on that little person, making him/her the center of a universe. But because everything seems to revolve around them, the child can't really imagine any universe in which their personal value is not the gravitational force around which everything circles.

This notion that one is at the center of all things must be disabused to enter adulthood, and that requires a Copernican shock of insight- a suddenly magnified view of the universe that starkly demonstrates how the sun, planets, and stars do not actually revolve around us.

Such shocks sometimes happen early in life due to a meteoric disaster that hits close to home, resetting the child's perspective about the primacy of their life. More commonly the shock is a slow rolling affair that chiefly begins when the child moves away from home and from dependence to assume the weight of full-time self-reliance. That eye opening shock steadily makes its impression as the intense gravity exerted by things outside their orbit is progressively experienced.

Either is a look through the telescope that pierces a sky clouded by naïve perceptions to bring the real universe into focus. We discover that the swirling universe features an infinite number of centers, a realization that puts the centrality of one's own value into question. And while this insight can be discomforting, as it was when Copernicus made his discoveries about the nature of heavenly bodies, it is also a profoundly freeing discovery. It frees the individual from the limits of childish, egocentric suppositions and opens the mind to the exploration of new spheres rather than remaining psychologically bound at the

 *PUT AWAY CHILDISH THINGS*
Shedding naive notions VS Chronic gullibility

center of just a few satellites. It reveals the give and take of all those gravitational forces, and the fact that one may increase their own pull only by creating value that is attractive to other bodies in the sky.

Realizing the Copernican truth that we are not the center of things is not a disappointment of youth. It is the stargate to adulthood, with all its demands and opportunities, that becomes real only when we see the universe clearly for the first time.

> "This is the true joy in life... being a force of Nature instead of a feverish selfish little clod of ailments and grievances complaining that the world will not devote itself to making you happy."
>
> *George Bernard Shaw*

Fixing Flats

A flat usually happens when it's pouring down rain and we're late for an appointment. The experienced reaction to this, one of life's many imperfect moments, is typically a feeling of annoyance and an exasperated huff. But to those who have been over-protected from life's common mishaps, the reaction can be something closer to a kind of righteous indignation.

Such bubble-wrapped souls contextualize all mishaps through the naïve supposition that all things in life should forever be convenient and well-functioning. After all, for them, life has always been so. But once the bubble-wrap has been removed through graduation to adulthood, the occurrence of less than convenient events can take them quite by surprise, rendering them shocked, frustrated, and even feeling somehow offended. Panic might even set in due to inexperience in dealing with such inconvenient troubles. In fact, these souls can whip themselves into quite a frenzy at the roadside.

That's a lot of emotional energy for a flat tire.

Perhaps this naïve attitude developed under the influence of helicopter parents who always kept discomfort at a distance, or due to the broader self-esteem movement that has insisted that the ego be protected from all bruises. In her book: *Free Range Kids*, Lenore Skenazy details with humor and practical insight the dangers of this philosophy and the contrasting power that children develop when allowed to take some bruises and resolve their own dilemmas instead. The Cleveland Clinic publication: *Could Your 'Helicopter Parenting' Actually Be Detrimental to Your Child's Development?* goes so far as to identify developmental milestones that children may miss when parenting becomes too overbearing. These include the loss of learning that would normally come via mistakes made, and a reduced ability for self-advocacy that would otherwise develop through the normal practice of standing up for oneself without parental intervention. Whatever the reason, such protected kids fail to develop the perspective and skills that would naturally come from suffering the difficult impacts and setbacks that life naturally brings.

When a tire goes flat, literally or metaphorically, it highlights what a foible all that bubble-wrapping of the child was. Life is an inherently messy affair characterized by universal inequity and chaotic problems. Messy blowouts of one kind or another abound and touch every life regardless of how protected that life may have been early on. But the sight of your car resting on the wheel rim looks quite unacceptably imperfect to the overprotected young person who has been scrupulously spared contact with such inevitable problems. A flat tire can cause an emotional blowout.

Would-be helicopter parents and self-esteem zealots would be wise to understand that the young must encounter problems and suffer losses to gain realistic perspective and to build the inner resilience and resourcefulness needed to resolve issues. Only through engagement with the world's messes can we learn to clean them up without a big fuss.

This takes practice, and best to practice on rather benign things (like fixing flats) so when a truly significant problem arises later, one is equipped to deal with it. So, rather than hovering above to circumvent every hard lesson, it's best to prepare young people for the future by assuring that some actual "flats" can happen to them early in life. Metaphorically, cancel the road-side assistance contract and convey key knowledge about how to use a lug wrench and a jack. Put the tools in their hands, not yours, and let them change some tires on their own.

Fixing flats builds realism, resourcefulness, resilience, and the earned self-esteem that comes only from handling problems yourself. With those tools in hand the young person is ready to cope with a world that will not protect him/her from the future troubles that are sure to come-far from the roadside.

PUT AWAY CHILDISH THINGS
Shedding naive notions VS Chronic gullibility

> *"... To grow up is to accept vulnerability... To be alive is to be vulnerable."*
>
> Madeleine L'Engle

Failure to Molt

Maturity comes only when the desire to grow overcomes the desire to fit in.

Of course, we all have a desire to fit in. But in youth that desire is quite intense and central to being. It's likely why kids dutifully go along with their peers' ideas, feelings, dress, attitudes, tastes, politics, mannerisms, language, and behaviors, regardless how naïve and silly those things may be. Conformance with peers wraps the child in a comforting, tight skin that, like swaddling a baby, relieves anxiety. It sooths some of the normal, anxiety-producing self-consciousness of youth and its attendant, outsized fear of judgement. You did it too. Remember the hair style you wore?

But to reach maturity we must molt that swaddled safety. To be mature is to think for oneself. (The hair style must go too.) Yet, some remain swaddled in a judgement-free, corset of conformity with prior youthful notions well past the normal age for molting. These would-be adults prefer its snug safety, not realizing how the restrictive skin stunts their growth by preventing development of the more mature perspectives that they might otherwise grow into.

This stunting can extend well into adult age because conforming with naïve notions just feels so warm and safe. Are you still zipped in? Do you still hold the same views in politics, about people and relationships, and possess the same attitudes as in the conformist youth of you and your peers. If so, it's unlikely because the youthful notions of the 18- or 21-year-old you were unassailably correct out of the box. You've simply failed to molt those conformist ideas and have unintentionally stunted your growth. You're still zipped inside a naïve conformist skin.

It's time to give the zipper a stronger tug. While you may feel vulnerable while molting the conformist skin, it's the only way to grow.

> "Don't let feelings guide your behavior.
> Let behavior shape your feelings."
>
> Dennis Praeger

Passionately Incompetent

People are not always good at what they are initially passionate about. Just watch one of those insipid talent shows where poor souls who are emphatically passionate about their art turn out to be quite pathetically terrible at it. Passion is certainly there, but clearly, talent is not the direct result of passionate pursuit.

If you are clumsy and uncoordinated by nature, evidenced by the fact that friends seem to have moved fragile items from their tables before your visit, then a career in ballet is not likely to be in the cards. Years of ballet lessons and passionate practice will likely improve performance, maybe even relieving those friends' anxiety about their delicate items when you stop by. But it's not going to turn you into a prima ballerina. That position will go to someone who started with strong, natural talent, then, standing atop that talent, developed it to even greater heights through years of hard work.

Fortunately, however, passion does naturally grow from exercising and developing the real talents that we do possess. We sometimes discover a talent by accident when we try something new or face a new challenge. Suddenly we find that we are good at something we'd hardly considered before. That discovery strikes a spark of interest that drives us to do that thing more and more. With focused attention our skill grows, transforming the spark of interest into the fire of passion that drives further learning and practice to create ever greater skill in a virtuous cycle: talent, prompting passion, prompting skill development, prompting more passion, and so on. But because this time the passion is grounded in innate talent, it drives to outcomes that are natural for the person. By contrast, passions that emerge outside the realm of talent try to force unnatural outcomes that will never be, regardless of how passionately one pursues it.

That is what makes the "follow your passion" advice so tragic. The person who is following an ungrounded passion to a dead-end surely possesses real talent for something else- but they are not developing that something else while they follow their ungrounded passion to nowhere.

Of course, it's difficult to know the difference between the passion that is grounded in talent and the passion that is not. That measure might be made according to how much you initially excel at the thing vs the amount you struggle with it. Others can also help gauge the situation because they see your talents without the confusion of feeling your passions.

In any case, put away the notion that any passionate pursuit will inevitably lead to greatness. It can only do so if built upon talent. So, the question is: Am I truly good at this, or do I just love it? If it's just something that you love, not grounded in recognizable talent, you can make it a wonderful hobby and continue to exercise your passion for it. But don't let obsession with hobbies stand in the way of creating that virtuous cycle of ever-increasing passion for that which you truly do have innate talent.

Only your well-grounded passion can be followed without fear that some talent show judge will suddenly press a giant buzzer to abruptly end your performance- and your passionate dream.

Based on wise insights of Mike Rowe

PUT AWAY CHILDISH THINGS
Shedding naive notions VS Chronic gullibility

> "I find television very educating. Every time somebody turns on the set, I go into the other room and read a book."
>
> Groucho Marx

Of Pride and Pretense

Actors portray fictional characters or attempt to recreate the personas of fascinating real people. The stories portrayed are written to be outsized and dramatic, so the actors' portrayals work to emphasize what is larger than life.

And we are dazzled. The realism and emotion of their performances draw us in with excitement and delight. In fact, we can be so taken in that we begin to perceive the actors themselves to be the characters who they made seem so real on-screen even though off-screen those actors are usually nothing like the people they portrayed. After all, playing a hero, or a brilliant scientist, or a wise sage doesn't convey those attributes to the actor. Still, fans often enthusiastically imagine the actors to be like their characters, or at least to be of the same caliber.

As do the actors themselves, apparently. Extrapolating from their brilliance on screen, many take great pride in pretending that they possess knowledge and wisdom, particularly in the social and political domains, that is clearly beyond them. Then too, a lifetime of pretending to be what one is not, cocooned within an industry that exists for the express purpose of delivering pretense, likely leaves the actor uniquely unqualified to speak to the nature of the real world and its problems. That's not where they live, and after all, the job is to pretend. As such, it is hard to imagine anyone so ill equipped to offer real-world insight than performers, nor anyone whose apparent earnestness could be more misleading.

WHEN MONKEYS FLY

Give performers their due within their prescribed role. But pay no attention to the views of those whose job it is to attract your attention and admiration via pure artifice. They have no idea what they are talking about.

PUT AWAY CHILDISH THINGS
Shedding naive notions VS Chronic gullibility

> "Too much of what is called 'education' is little more than an expensive isolation from reality."
>
> Thomas Sowell

Peter Pan on Campus

At many institutions, college seems to be increasingly treated as the embodiment of a children's book- a delightful pretend world for children who don't want to grow up. Its protective bubble is filled with lovely accommodations, an endless bounty of yummy food prepared for students, exotic athletic facilities and play areas, activist protection against the hearing of words that might possibly offend, encouragement in even the most juvenile notions, and safe spaces with fluffy toys to cuddle. It's the story of Never Land without the scary parts.

Certainly, there is study and testing to endure, and that is quite intense and serious. In fact, within the STEM fields pedagogy is more robust and challenging today than ever. Yet, while college has always offered the opportunity for fun, the contemporary academy experience seems, overall, less a preparation for future life than a denial of it. Tiny insults are elevated to the highest threat level *("I think he/she might have just made a micro aggressive remark to me!")*. Alternate points of view are vilified and those holding such perspectives are banned from expressing their views, *("Words are violence!")*. Revisionist history and grievance studies abound, presenting students with a decidedly contrived view of the world. This campus storybook shifts focus from the real to the fanciful while also holding the normal discomforts and responsibilities of adult life at bay. Too often, it thereby fails to prepare students for the real-life difficulties just outside the campus grounds.

There, Captain Hook waits, ready to administer a dose of scary reality far more terrible than a microaggression. College should prepare students for that reality by requiring that they hear differing ideas, not run away from them, that they put minor insult and conflict in its proper perspective, and that they learn the full context of history, not just grievance-based cherry pickings that paint everyone as either victim or oppressor. Students need to acquire the balanced knowledge and personal resilience needed to face the good Captain once they exit the doors of the academy.

But universities are unlikely to change these storybook aberrations anytime soon. They are part and parcel of the institutions' ideology and business model. So, students, you must take your preparation for Captain Hook's domain into your own hands. Put away the childish things of the academy and seek a more grown-up understanding of the world. The people outside will not be like your professors and peers, and the rules will not follow the campus handbook. It is an indelicate and difficult world into which you will graduate, for which you must be realistically prepared. There will be no imaginary Never Land safe space to retreat into when things get scary.

Captain Hook doesn't care if he frightens you.

PUT AWAY CHILDISH THINGS
Shedding naive notions VS Chronic gullibility

> *"In theory there is no difference between theory and practice. In practice there is."*
>
> Yogi Berra

Theoretically Infatuated

Some people become infatuated by attractive-sounding sociopolitical ideas. Sometimes the infatuation begins with childhood indoctrination, but often it comes at university, a place where gaining knowledge seems to take second priority to gaining the "right" theoretical points of view. Among naïve college students the appeal of such theories is easy to understand – they sound good to the inexperienced mind and seem to offer comprehensible pat answers to vexing issues. There's just one problem. While they work in theory, in practice most fail miserably.

Still, the theories are dearly loved for the lovely theoretical notions they represent- the romantic future the theory promises. So, they are romanticized by their lovers who also work to obfuscate any evidence of the theory's faults, telling little lies to sustain the romance. It's rather like the obsession that holds the naïve lover in a relationship with an abusive boyfriend or girlfriend. The obvious failings of their mate are always excused to circumstances or to matters of interpretation. "Next time," insists the naïve lover, "things will be different. If I just stick with them, they'll change."

They won't.

Flawed sociopolitical theories don't change either. Like the abusive lover, they solicitously ingratiate themselves during the courtship period with bright promises that the naïve are more than willing to believe, only revealing a darker side once the romance has secured its hold. At that point the infatuated begin to obscure the newly visible failings of their beloved theory by ignoring the signals and doubling down on their belief in its righteousness and success. As in the Texas Sharpshooter fallacy, the infatuated draw concentric circles around the errant bullet hole of their beloved theory and declare it has hit the bullseye. Then, if called on the trick, they reflexively attack those who dare question the validity of their passion, insisting that others "just don't understand".

This infatuation is irrational and fierce.

Stubborn allegiance to an abusive lover or to recognizably flawed theories is not the product of a rational process. It is merely wishful thinking acting out- a blinding desire to believe that what seemed to offer such promise can be, despite all evidence to the contrary. Beloved theories die very hard. But the loved theory and its fanaticized future represents the most tragic kind of love. It is the love of something that will never be that takes the place of something real that might have been.

When It's Not Academic
If you were sick, would you go to see an experienced, practicing physician or someone who is a brilliant student of medical science but who has never touched a patient?

PUT AWAY CHILDISH THINGS
Shedding naive notions VS Chronic gullibility

> *"Some people get an education without going to college. The rest get it after they get out."*
>
> Mark Twain

The Unschooled Harvest

Wisdom doesn't grow from the proper use of grammar and vocabulary, from the understanding of math and science, nor upon deep knowledge of other topics that one can acquire in school. As valuable as those things are, harvesting wisdom is tougher than acquiring such learnings.

Wisdom comes from the lived experience that steadily builds an understanding of patterns among people and circumstances. It can be acquired through one's own experience or conveyed through stories told by others meant to express wise lessons learned. Harvested vine by vine, it lets you recognize situations that fit the pattern of something that doesn't turn out well- or does turn out well- or that requires some kind of action to influence the outcome. Such insights come from connecting the dots of growing experience to understand their patterns, and we call that experience-derived insight: wisdom.

This means that knowledge alone will not make you wise. Of course, many who possess a lot of knowledge like to think of themselves as being wise. But they've missed the point and, ironically, their self-important attitude about expertise can block the acquisition of life's wisdom. One must possess enough humility to recognize that the roots of wisdom grow deeper than that of current knowledge. Yet great knowledge often pushes humility out of its way. Which means that less educated folks may just understand how to connect life's dots better than the exalted professor.

While much wisdom has been crystallized by a lot of rather well-educated people, (several of whom are quoted in this book), most of life's practical wisdom can be found embodied in rather ordinary people who gleaned it from natural sources. Such wisdom, often quite old, is sometimes sharpened and passed on by great minds through the tales they write. Unsurprisingly, those tales often concern the lives of ordinary people.

But young people who possess newly harvested knowledge are predisposed to reject anything old under the assumption that it must be outdated. Surely the newest thinking is the best. Yet, old and world-worn insights are like fine, red wine- improved by age. True wisdom grows on old vines through many seasons of experience and trial, then stands the test of time as it ages to full maturity. These are the very insights that fresh knowledge, however exalted, cannot provide. Wisdom takes time. So, one must remain open to insights that do not have a contemporary ring to them, in fact, especially if they don't.

To harvest the dot-connecting wisdom of old, put aside the freshness bias and tune your palate for the time-tested wisdom that often exudes from classic stories, is bound into traditions, and yes, is directly spoken and demonstrated by those who came before you- regardless of their schooling. These should be your mentors, offering life's most useful and lasting insights, and illustrating how to wisely connect the dots of your own experiences as those experiences grow through time.

It's Concerning

Immature people tend to have a high level of concern for others' transitory emotions, but relatively less real concern for others' overall wellbeing.

By contrast, mature people tend to have a high level of concern for the wellbeing of others, but relatively low concern for transitory emotions.

PUT AWAY CHILDISH THINGS
Shedding naive notions VS Chronic gullibility

> "To be mature means to face, and not evade, every fresh crisis that comes."

Fritz Kunkel

Cold Water

If you use the currently popular term "adulting" to describe your occasional foray into the responsible waters of adulthood, that snarky attitude is forestalling your necessary departure from childhood.

It is only when we fully let go of childhood that we discover that adulthood's requirement for self-reliance, planning, accountability, and selflessness is not just something to be played at periodically. It is so deeply enriching and freeing that it deserves one's full commitment, even if the dive into that pool seems shockingly cold at first.

But it's no good just dipping in your toes occasionally, then running away from the water's edge. You must fully commit by jumping in and swimming that sea. Don't worry. You'll shake off the cold and discover that not only is the water "fine", it is also fantastically deep, and broad, and full of opportunity.

But to discover this you'll have to dive- headfirst.

> "Truth is the torch that gleams through
> the fog without dispelling it."
>
> Claude Adrien Helvetius

A Torch to Carry

The torch of Western civilization has lighted the way through earthly darkness for a few centuries now. It cast that glow by developing the economic mechanisms that have lifted billions from poverty; establishing systems of legal justice that enable fair treatment for all under the law; spawning a body of art, literature, and music of unparalleled fineness that informs and inspires the human spirit; contributing scientific and technological advances that have simultaneously reduced suffering and expanded our human capabilities in astonishing ways; and so much more. All were built upon the West's shining principles that include empiricism, skepticism, liberalism, individualism, and Judeo-Christian morality. Other cultures have made magnificent contributions to be sure. But, despite its horrible mistakes, the West's glittering positive impact on human flourishing has been more brilliant than any other source.

If your education has led you to think that the Western world is the seat of oppression, it has failed to provide a balanced view. A shallow focus upon only the West's mistakes can only yield victim-centered interpretations of its past, literature, and structures rather than a clear and complete view in perspective. Notice that the purveyors of such superficial views never contextualize their interpretations by positing the question: Compared to what? That is the question that allows us to set aside naïve comparisons to eutopia so we may examine the real.

Thus, those who educate and comment must be able and inclined to place events in relevant context. Without context, ("Compared to what?"), only indoctrination remains, delivered by one-eyed zealots who focus solely upon the West's failings. Clearly, the failings are there, but to see with perspective we must keep one eye on the failings and the other on the remarkable successes. With balanced perspective we understand that the contemporary outrage with the West that cries: "Burn it all down!" is the product of half-blinded minds.

This scotoma is promulgated through the reinterpretation and rewriting of history and via myriad ideologies and causes proffered by academics, media, and search engines- often promoted with popular, social taglines. So, seeing with perspective requires the seeking out of literature and histories that haven't yet suffered a one-eyed rewrite to suit current social fashions. You want the truth- not just the currently trending "truth". That more balanced view, gained from two-eyed perspective, progressively reveals that, (adapting Churchill): Western civilization is the worst civilization in the world- except for all the others.

The West's philosophy is a torch worth carrying because it has, and does, illuminate the way by which human beings may best pursue individual happiness, fulfillment, and the flourishing of all people. Closing one or both eyes to its brilliance is what strikes the careless match that would burn down all the best that humanity has been able to muster.

But when all has been burned, so too will be the torch, and we return to darkness.

LANDING

Put Away Childish Things
Shedding naive notions VS Chronic gullibility

There is nothing more ugly than a 30-year-old child.

Though many well-meaning people may have tried to protect you from life's harsher realities, you must reject the comfort of the safe space and face the world's difficulties with courage and resolve. Life's experiences necessarily include struggles and disappointments and painful tragedies. Perpetual protection from these only preserves a childish outlook- a world of pretty theories and platitudes upon which no wise reality can be built.

Glinda knew that Dorothy needed to "learn it for herself", through difficult experience. Consider your own experience. What lessons have you learned from your failures and despairs that have opened your eyes to what works and what doesn't? The view may not have been pretty, but it offered a real foundation on which to stand, not just squishy platitudes about the way things "should" be.

Unwrapping the protective bubble of naïve notions empowers you to understand, embrace, and build upon the best that the world has been able to muster, even with its flaws. From this understanding, wisdom grows.

The future does not belong to the children. It belongs to children who become grown-ups.

PUT AWAY CHILDISH THINGS
Shedding naive notions VS Chronic gullibility

> *"Childish fantasy, like the sheath over the bud, not only protects but curbs the terrible budding spirit, protects not only innocence from the world, but the world from the power of innocence."*
>
> Elizabeth Bowen

WHEN MONKEYS FLY

Treasure Individuals
Celebrating individuality VS Identity politics

Dorothy learned to cherish each of her new friends, not for what they seemed to be, but for what they truly were at heart. That depth is essential to form real relationships, whether romantic, friend, family, colleague, or fellow traveler. Yet, in our foolish world we too often see only the category or belief to which a person belongs, failing to invest the time and patience needed to understand the full depth of others with more nuance. Much easier to resort to identity politics.

On this flight we look at positive habits that build relationship and at the ways we sometimes fail those relationships. When that happens, we may use the trusty line: "It's not you it's me" to soften the blow. (It's also a pretty good punchline.) But in reality, sometimes it's you and sometimes it's me. Yet it is only by seeing the true nature of relationship and of the individuals involved can human connections form or fail with honesty (even those with lions, scarecrows, and tin men.)

WHEN MONKEYS FLY

This is a call to embrace the habit of treasuring people for ALL their unique attributes so we may embrace those individuals honestly and fully. We must treasure individuals, not identities.

> *"Everyone you meet is fighting a battle you
> know nothing about. Be Kind. Always"*
>
> Unknown

Abusing Demographics

Everyone seems to speak authoritatively about the behaviors and attitudes of people who fit within any demographic group. Politicians and commentators practically make their living by selling their views on the characteristics of each demographic, while lay people sling demographic-speak matter-of-factly to sound in the know. Except, that is, when they proceed to explain how they themselves don't really fit the common mold of their own demographic group. Suddenly, demographics don't tell the real story.

Which is exactly correct, of course. Individuals are simply not defined by the demographic labels that attach to them. The lives and backgrounds of individual human beings are complex and unique. Each has their own distinct attributes, histories, and circumstances that defy the average of any group. So, despite whatever the demographics may suggest about the average attitudes and behaviors of its members, everyone has faced unique hardships, challenges, tragedies, victories, and jackpots that we simply can't know from the group-level statistics.

This fact seems to elude many of us, particularly those who make their living, in part, by exercising demographic-speak with great authority. They smugly assume that each member of the demographic group can be expected to exhibit similar behaviors and attitudes, effectively objectifying the individual by ignoring the myriad factors that contribute to individual characteristics. This lazy thinking is used to frame people with blanket labels like "advantaged" or "disadvantaged" while assigning blanket blame or issuing blanket immunity based upon those labels.

Yet, even the most apparently fortunate ("advantaged") person may well have suffered crushing blows that we know nothing about: Perhaps their most loved one is suffering from cancer, perhaps they had a child die, perhaps they once lost everything they had to an unscrupulous person, perhaps they were the child of an alcoholic, perhaps they've been abused, perhaps they've received a dire medical diagnosis, perhaps they are fighting depression, perhaps they have a child in trouble or care for a parent with Alzheimer's disease, perhaps, perhaps, perhaps... You just can't know purely on the basis of their demographics.

Which begs the question: Just which members of any demographic group deserve to be treated in some particular way based purely upon a demographic attribute they have? What individual hardships or windfalls are not being accounted for by that person's demographic profile? Shouldn't we allow for the possibility that even the person who we presume needs no sympathy may well suffer from severe, unseen, and undeclared misfortunes? Are we to treat human beings as though there are simply interchangeable members of an animal herd characterized only by the pattern on their hide?

To test if your thinking is based upon such superficial distinctions, flip the demographics of the person you are judging. If you would treat that person differently were their demographics different, you are clearly blind to the distinctive elements of their individual humanity. You are lazily dismissing their uniqueness and the vital realities that are unrevealed by mere demographics. You are abusing demographics.

Through such superficial judgement we inflict pain and damage by villainizing or patronizing those who deserve neither, usually carried out under the banner of "good intentions." Breaking this pattern requires respect for the individual irrespective of the demographic group to which they belong.

TREASURE INDIVIDUALS
Celebrating individuality vs Identity politics

The practice of cherishing individuals, not groups, avoids the casual damage that labels inflict, and serves to bolster the dignity of all.

Including you.

> *"Most of us must learn to love people and use things rather than loving things and using people."*
>
> Roy T. Bennett

Beyond Average

Take this idea about the abuse of demographics a step further. Even when statistics can express the average attributes of a group, those averages cannot be used to assess an individual member of that group.

The commonly bell-curve shaped distributions of group characteristics let us speak of the typical or average characteristics of the group as a whole. For example, we might assess height across populations and find that, on average, the Dutch are quite tall indeed.

But represented on the Dutch bell-curve of height there are many individuals who are not typical for the group. Some are much shorter than average and some much taller. Thus, the fat part of the bell represents only the majority of group members (quite tall), while its trailing edges represent the very real, though smaller number of group members who possess more or less of the characteristic (tallness). The Dutch are rather tall on average, but they are not all the same.

Individuals are variously distributed along the curve of any characteristic, but we can't know where on the curve any given individual falls without individually assessing that individual. That may be easy to accomplish in the case of height but is more complex with less visible attributes such as attitudes and beliefs. As in the case of height, though we may find a prevalent viewpoint within a particular group it is not possible to assign that viewpoint to any individual member of the group without taking their individual measure. That individual may be an outlier- situated on a trailing end of the bell curve. Blindly assuming that they hold the average viewpoint ignores the mathematical reality of the distribution curve. It discounts the

TREASURE INDIVIDUALS
Celebrating individuality vs Identity politics

uniqueness of that individual human being in a uniquely dehumanizing act. None of us would like to be so impersonally judged.

Assuming that an individual is defined by the average of their group is both a factual error and a moral one. Every person is, in their own ways, beyond average.

> *"If you don't stand for something,
> you'll fall for anything"*
>
> Unknown

Do Judge

When people issue the popular edict: "Don't Judge!", what they really mean, or should mean, is: "Don't judge superficially."

We all make judgements throughout the day as we assess the world around us. As pointed out by Harvard psychologist Amy Cuddy, an expert in first impressions, what seems to be a split-second judgement of someone is just you asking yourself two quick things: "Can I trust this person", and "should I respect this person?" She further points out that we form beliefs based upon the repetition of certain stimuli that we find are associated with certain traits. As such we intuitively form judgements based on factors such as appearance, sociability, and demonstrated morality as generalized from experience.

We apply this kind of experience-based quick judgement to all kinds of practical matters day-to-day: Is this event a positive or a negative for me? Is this person a danger or an ally? Can I eat this? Can I trust this organization? Will this book be worth my time? (Hopefully, you judge it to be so.)

Judgement is a necessary survival skill. It is the tool we use to determine how to conduct our lives within a world that is filled with potential risks. It is baked into our DNA. If it were not, our species wouldn't still be here, having long-ago been killed-off by dangers that penetrated a judgement-free outlook. Quite simply, we must judge to both survive and to thrive.

However, we should not judge superficially, particularly people (as in the old saw about judging a book by its cover.) Beneath the superficial, we often find great depth, unexpected dimensions, and fascinating perspective in others- a wealth of experience and insight to learn from.

But once you've gotten below the superficial, you most definitely must judge what you find, even if you wisely keep that judgement to yourself.

> "Nature gave men two ends - one to sit on and one to think with. Ever since then man's success or failure has been dependent on the one he used most."

George Ross Kirkpatrick

Tight Lipped

The mouth is a two-way portal, and it can get us into trouble in either direction:

> What goes in determines how healthy your body can be.

> What comes out determines how healthy your relationships can be.

We all know people who have trouble with one direction or the other, and sometimes both. Remaining a bit more tight-lipped would be good for many of us, facilitating our ability to appear both thinner and less vapid as a result.

> *"To love is to will the good of the other, as other. Love is not restful nor sentimental in illusions, but watchful, alert, and ready to follow evidence. It seeks the real as lungs crave air."*
>
> Michael Novak

Good for Who?

When you do something that will be good for you, you reap the benefit, usually in the long term. Unfortunately, bad-for-you things are immediate, abundant, accessible, and have the nasty trait of making you feel really good right now. That effect is so compelling that we often ignore the known negative consequences to gain the immediate dopamine hit that comes with a bad act. Even when conscious of the negatives we tend to dismiss their distant impacts by imagining that those impacts will never materialize or can be dispensed expeditiously if they do.

But the crucial element that such short-sighted gratification ignores is the impact that our bad-for-you acts have on the loving people who only want the best for us. When they see our ill-considered actions, they can't ignore or dismiss the negative consequences that will come to the person they love. And it hurts them.

But the corollary action of committing good-for-you things not only reaps long-term benefits for oneself, it also delivers immediate benefits to those loving people around you. They are joyful at foreseeing the wonderful outcomes on their way to something they love.

You.

Unlovable Neighbors

Some neighbors are easy to love, while others seem hell bent on irritating you to the point of distraction. Fortunately, you don't have to actually feel love for your neighbor to love your neighbor.

Love for your neighbor, regardless of their level of lovability, is expressed in simple acts of kindness: a simple kind word, or lending a hand, or creating some small opportunity that the other person can leverage to better their own life. Loving your neighbor does not require you to feel love, it only requires you to express love through tangible acts. And you can do that even when you just don't feel it.

Successful relationships are not built only upon our feelings in any case. They are built upon our deeds. They grow from the positive things you do and the negative things you don't do, irrespective of your feelings. Taking positive action even when you don't "feel it" is the progenitor of positive relationship and the route to more positive feeling.

So, it simply doesn't matter whether you feel love for your neighbor. As that neighbor benefits from the small, positive actions you take toward them you build both a more positive relationship with them and expand the most positive, loving parts within yourself.

Though you may never feel love for the neighbor who is always playing loud music at 1AM, through simple acts you can nevertheless help them to feel just a little bit loved and, in the process, find that you love yourself just a little bit more too.

It might even get the volume turned down.

TREASURE INDIVIDUALS
Celebrating individuality vs Identity politics

> "Don't win the argument and lose the relationship"
>
> Lauren Green

The Greater Angel of Relationship

Recall those old movies in which a character who is deliberating a difficult dilemma is shown in close-up with a tiny angel on one shoulder and a devil on the other. The two argue their opposing points of view about what action should be taken while the character's head swivels back and forth between them, confusedly struggling to resolve which advice to follow.

Our dilemmas often center on the ordinary conflicts that arise between people. When they do, that shoulder devil always seems to goad us into approaches that damage relationships rather than building them: demeaning the other's views to elevate our own by comparison, chastising the other to beat them into submission, and if all else fails, resenting the other for who and what they are.

But the angel has another way:

> Educate rather than demean. In the process you might even learn something yourself.
>
> Encourage rather than chastise. This opens the opportunity to lead others to better pursuits rather than merely creating opposition.
>
> Enjoy rather than resent. Adopt the first two entreaties and the third comes naturally.

Personally Apolitical

When political differences enter the personal sphere, we risk pitting the two against each other. Too often people back away from personal relationships with friends and family to avoid the conflict of their opposing political views. *"Oh God, we just can't invite Uncle Charlie. You know who he supports!"*

If we let that happen, we effectively subjugate our love for people to the political positions we espouse. We demonstrate that we care less for those people than we do for our own political stance. It is a tragic display of ideological narcissism.

Of course, there are techniques to more safely manage highly charged discussions as described by author and clinical psychologist Eileen Kennedy-Moore. Her suggestions include: Keep it friendly by skipping the insults and sarcasm; Be curious; Ask questions to seek understanding; Acknowledge good points when you can and; Be humble by aiming for understanding, not victory. The victories won over friends and family are pyrrhic by nature, in any case.

Still, sometimes political bridges simply can't be built with friends or family members. When they cannot, the alternative to cutting off the people in your life is to instead make a cutline between the political and the personal. These folks are connected to you for good reason through bond of friendship or family bond. Friends became friends because that connection ran deep. Does your attachment lose its importance because political views surface? Family being family, the connection is innate and unavoidable despite clashes of political views.

But by putting political issues and conflicts on one side of that cutline instead of cutting off the people, you can enjoy all the wonderful things that friends and family members offer apart from their political views. And those are the things that count most- their humor, knowledge, experiences, stories, interests and, of course, your shared affection. What's more, by preserving relationships in this way you also reserve

the opportunity to engage over politics at a future, more opportune time.

Or not.

We may certainly embrace our politics with great passion. But it is only wise to cherish one's friends and family with even greater passion. Charlie will be your uncle regardless of how his or your political views may evolve. Save his seat at the table. He's still got a few great stories to tell. And despite your differences, it's very likely that you still occupy a warm place in his heart. Cherish that over your politics.

> *"A happy marriage is the union of two good forgivers."*
>
> Ruth Graham

Love of Words

Love is not merely a word nor a feeling. It is an action.

Incessantly saying "I love you" is not love. Doing the grocery shopping when it's not your turn is love.

Marital Glue

Marriage requires two components to make it stick.

Part one: Romantic Love- which provides passion and commitment.

Part two: Friendship- which provides compatibility, teamwork, and breathing room.

Love without friendship is impractical and stifling. Friendship without romantic love is just, well... friendship. We need both to make a marriage work.

As much as we are told that love conquers all, turns out that it doesn't conquer the day-to-day friction that results when two people try to cooperate over the chores. Life involves a lot of drudgery, challenges, and decisions that your mate (the friend part) will work with you to get through. Similarly, over time, life also tends to be both numbing and filled with distracting alternatives which your mate (the romantic part) will contravene with sparkle and passion.

The state of love is what we drive for and often why we're driving in the first place. It can give us purpose and a soulful warmth that makes it all worthwhile. But friendship is how we pull it off- how we cooperate and find fun in the twists and turns and tedium throughout the drive. Friendship lets us harmoniously and happily navigate the obstacles.

A marriage with both components is glued together. If there is just one component in place, you've got a Sticky Note.

When "Yes" Means "Yes"

Before some college administrators decided that young women and men should have to sign a declaration of consent prior to engaging in sexual activity with a partner, society had a much more robust and meaningful process in place. It was called marriage.

In that day, couples largely waited until after marriage to have sex. The courtship, engagement and wedding planning were all part of a period during which both parties could consider the option with a clear head as they also took the time to build a strong relationship in love and friendship. The marriage itself was witnessed by family and friends in an event that took months to plan and was full of rituals and pledges. There simply could be no more definitive "yes" to the coupling of two people.

Yet now, many seek to replace this traditional and uniquely definitive "yes" with sterile and dehumanizing substitutes (e.g.: "sexual consent contracts"), all the while tossing off abstinence before marriage as a quaint, old oddity. It is quaint, of course, and by today's standards quite odd. But what of the contemporary substitute?

The so called "sexual consent contract" is certainly not quaint, in fact, it is thoroughly modern: "Just check the box that says you consent to this User Agreement and let's get started!" But it also sadly documents the nature of the relationship- both parties are "using" one another under legal agreement. It is not really a relationship at all. It's a transaction.

How romantic.

Opening Doors

When a man opens the car door for his wife or girlfriend, both understand that the act is purely unnecessary. She doesn't need him to open that door for her, not in the least. She knows this and he knows it too. He fully understands that she quite ably opens the car door for herself every single day without his assistance.

But the fact that both parties understand that the act is completely unnecessary is exactly what makes it a pure gesture of caring. He is demonstrating in this tiny way that he cherishes her so much that he'll even perform an utterly unnecessary act of courtesy on her behalf.

The woman receiving this courtesy can react in either of two ways: she can perceive it as a demonstration of caring or can perceive it as an act of dominance. Now, as an act of dominance, it's pretty lame, but as an act of caring, it's pretty nice. Better for both parties, and for the relationship, to give and take it as an act of caring that reinforces the best in the relationship.

The unnecessary nature of an unnecessary act of service is what makes it so necessarily meaningful. If taken the right way, it can do more than open doors. It can help open hearts.

LANDING

Treasure Individuals
Celebrating individuality vs Identity politics

Dehumanization is heart wrenching whether experienced directly or observed from afar. It is so because we instinctively understand the sanctity of the individual human life- the fact that we are not merely interchangeable members of one herd or another, but that we are each quite different despite shared attributes. So, it is only through a perverse aberration in that instinct that we dehumanize individuals or groups, usually prompted by tribalism or selfish convenience and sometimes simply to virtue-signal, (such as the disparaging of one's own demographic group.)

The Wizard understood that each member of Dorothy's band of travelers was not merely the label attached to them, even if they attached the label to themself. He saw beneath the superficial to understand the individual qualities of Scarecrow, Tin Man, and Lion, then celebrated those deeper attributes with awards that acknowledged them.

Consider your own experience. Recall an occasion when others characterized you based only upon your membership in a group or around a singular trait. Remember how diminished you felt when all the richness of your life experience and identity was reduced to a single attribute? That's identity politics at work.

In the most practical way, each person deserves the dignity of being treated as an individual because it is only as individuals that we may be fairly judged or rightly loved. Fair judgement is not based upon superficial characteristics, group membership, or expressed intentions. Fair judgement of any individual can only be based upon the demonstrated merit of the individual. In a similar way, authentic love can only be directed to particular individuals, spurred by the particular merits and actions of those individuals. So, we love each person quite differently and express that love through our own actions ranging from simple kindness to profound commitment.

In the final analysis, it is only between individuals that honest assessment can happen or that true relationship can form or fail. Whichever party may be to blame for a relationship failure, you must never let it fail for lack of seeing the individual apart from the crowd nor for lack of the effort necessary to actualize what love there might be.

Keep the wise habit of treasuring the individual. If you fail in this matter, then it truly was you, not me.

TREASURE INDIVIDUALS
Celebrating individuality vs Identity politics

*"Be strong, but kind.
Be kind, but strong."*

WHEN MONKEYS FLY

Live Consciously
Paying attention to the real VS Screen-numbed diversion

Dorothy was knocked unconscious and dreamt her way through the magical land of Oz, oblivious to the fact that the very home to which she desperately wanted to return was actually all around her at every moment.

In this flight we look at the ways that too many of us live in a similarly dreamy and shall we say: Zombie state, glued to colorful screens, obsessed by attention getting, or merely by allowing ourselves to be subsumed into a zombie-like herd of one kind or another. We fail to live consciously in the world around us because we are absorbed in other little worlds instead.

Alas, this behavior is pervasive in our foolish world. Once at a restaurant I tried to gather the attention of everyone sitting around the table. In the dim room all faces were illuminated by the unnatural glow of small screens. They were transfixed and I realized with a certain horror that my human companions no longer existed. I was sitting at a table with

WHEN MONKEYS FLY

the living dead, a pod of screen Zombies who were largely unaware of their surroundings and companions.

Should I beat a hasty retreat, or stay amongst the Zombie hoard?

I was hungry. I stayed. But effectively, I ate alone.

 *LIVE CONSCIOUSLY*
Paying attention to the real VS Screen-numbed diversion

> "I have a very strong feeling that the opposite of love is not hate - it's apathy. It's not giving a damn."
>
> Leo Buscaglia

Spending Time with Zombies

The undead don't notice much, don't make eye contact, and don't talk much either. They seem to live only within their own little bubble of consciousness and generally aren't much fun to be around. They are not like the people we knew while they were alive. They're different as zombies.

Of course, while zombies lack normal, human attention and engagement, they are terrifically sensitive to the slightest hint of human prey nearby. Their heads jerk in reflexive response to the sound of any potential feast, then maniacally follow the signal to gorge themselves. Zombies are single-minded that way.

Spending time with someone who repeatedly dips their head into their phone is rather like spending time with a zombie. The phone zombie lusts for the next, tiny dopamine hit generated by something novel on their phone. Their head jerks in reflexive response to any digital alert sound, and once again they are on the hunt... not talking much, not making eye contact, not noticing things in the physical world around them, living only in their own little bubble of consciousness and certainly not much fun to be around. They are not like the people we knew while they were alive.

The saddest part of the zombie transition is the fact that these were once humans who we loved and loved to be with. But once turned into zombies that connection wanes as we come to realize that their endless, dark lust has overtaken the former power of our love.

WHEN MONKEYS FLY

More than anything, zombies make us sad.

LIVE CONSCIOUSLY
Paying attention to the real VS Screen-numbed diversion

> *"Screens are often used merely as chewing gum for the mind"*

Chewing Gum

Time spent on screens can be as habitual and unfulfilling as gum chewing- both being a repetitious act of consumption that delivers flavor but no nutrition. Consider the nonstop devouring of sensationalistic news reporting, teeth-gnashing social media ingestion, gorging on entertainment or gaming, the gnawing behaviors of online surfing and shopping, and innumerable other such chewing motions.

Taken in smaller bites these time-filling activities are relatively benign. But heavy consumption isn't undertaken merely to fill time. It is an attempt to fill an inner void, the one left by a lack of fulfillment that likely began with a shortfall of purpose. This is an innermost void that expands when you realize that you are not getting the best from yourself, that your potential is not being exploited, and that you are not growing either in your career, your relationships, your health, your intellect, or your spirit. Sometimes it's just one of these deficits, but it may be all of them at once, leaving a yawning void that mere chewing gum cannot possibly fill. Like an empty belly, this void aches to be nourished by something more substantial.

Gum chewing distractions only distract us from better uses of time, keeping us from gathering the nutrients of purpose, effort, and fulfillment we so desperately need. There is good evidence of this effect. A meta-analysis of 158 studies concerning time management was published in 2021, (*Does time management work?* Aeon, Faber, Panaccio). The researchers found that effective use of time management enhances our sense of wellbeing, particularly that of life satisfaction. When we reduce time-wasting activities, we feel better about our lives and that feeling comes regardless of our circumstances.

WHEN MONKEYS FLY

The evidence indicates that we feel greater life satisfaction simply by using time productively rather than merely chewing it up.

But gum is sticky stuff and hard to get rid of. Hard to forgo its immediate gratification- that burst of flavor that drives you to grab one fresh stick after another. Yet saying "no" to mindless masticating frees both brain and time to cook up something far more nourishing. That more gratifying meal starts with a menu of purpose that leads to courses of effort that deliver growth in your career, relationships, health, intellect, spirit, and more; growth into the kind of person who you can admire and respect because that person lives a life of purposeful action, not merely monotonous chewing.

Spit out the gum and start cooking.

LIVE CONSCIOUSLY
Paying attention to the real VS Screen-numbed diversion

> *"To be yourself in a world that is constantly trying to make you something else is the greatest accomplishment."*
>
> *Ralph Waldo Emerson*

Pull the Plug

Once, I cut off my television's plug. This was way back in the pre-streaming, pre-smart phone days. I'd developed a habit turning on the TV after coming home from work to decompress for a few minutes. But there were so many channels to view that I often became entranced, scrolling through channel after channel in an endless carousel, or captured for hours in one program after another. When eventually my trance was broken, I felt disgusted about the time I'd wasted- the failure to make progress on something, anything, had been squandered on mind-numbed viewing. Yet the next day I'd press the ON button again, and again become entranced as hours passed.

One day, I'd finally had enough self-disgust over my TV watching. I came home that evening and instead of hitting the ON button, I pulled furniture away from the wall, found the TV's power cable, took out my diagonal wire cutters, and cut off the TV's plug. Problem solved.

Today the temptation of media is one-thousand-fold stronger not only due to the far more extensive range of content available, but because it's available on so many devices that are all around us and in our pockets. Worse, many of those devices are wireless. There isn't even a plug to cut.

This constant connection to devices and the content they emit exerts a powerful impact on us. It steals not only time that could be better used but actively detracts from our relationships. Habitual screen swiping that serves to quickly bring into view the next message or media clip is reflexively applied to people too, swiping away our attention to them as the next digital blip comes on screen. Our human connection becomes an interrupted, disjointed muddle, like an internet router that needs a restart. With a router, you disconnect to stop its stuttering, then reconnect to try again. Disconnecting is curative.

Disconnecting from the internet works not just for routers but for human beings as well, rendering an improvement in mental health. A study conducted by psychologist Melissa G. Hunt, published in the *Journal of Social and Clinical Psychology* found that participants who limited their consumption of popular social media tools to 30 minutes per day felt significantly better, reporting reduced depression, loneliness, and a reduction of their "fear of missing out," (FOMO.) Disconnecting is curative.

But limits are hard to self-regulate as I discovered long ago with my TV. Going cold turkey by cutting the plug as I did, or at least pulling it out of the wall, creates a much more definitive barrier to one's old habit. And pulling the plug is something that you can easily try out over the course of a weekend to test its impact. Here is the experiment: Pick a weekend during which you will completely disconnect from the constant, digital stream for those two weekend days. No mobile phone, tablet, computer, electronic games, TV, radio, streaming media... anything stuffed with microchips whether it has a plug or not. Yes, this seems a bit frightening at first (that's your FOMO showing up), but you CAN do it for two days.

During those days you will find that you have gained a significant amount of extra time and attention that you may then give to things not on screen. Use that time to engage in direct, human-to-human interaction or in solitary pursuits. Talk to people; do a hobby; play cards; workout; read a book; work on a project; etc. You decide just what to do with all the extra time that you have.

Be sure to take notice of how you feel about those activities and about yourself over the weekend. Your increased face-to-face, empathetic

LIVE CONSCIOUSLY
Paying attention to the real VS Screen-numbed diversion

connection with other humans will likely have a powerful, comforting effect. Even your solitary activities will create deeper connection with a human, (yourself), by focusing and calming the mind of that human. The stuttering bad connection you had to people while all the electronics were glowing in your face fades away while the glowing faces of people come into better focus. You will have experienced a reset of your humanity.

When your two-day experiment is over you can go back to the screens and resume the relentless noise of digital life. But once you've glimpsed the other side of the digital divide you're going to want to return. You're going to want to find that clarity of human connection again. You're going to want the quiet to hear your own thoughts again. You're going to want the glow of those faces met eye to eye at a deliberate pace, not just in glances over a screen. But the digital deluge is relentless and urgent and endlessly attention-grabbing. So how will you find the time again?

Schedule it. Put another reboot weekend on the calendar, and perhaps another after that. Or perhaps set a daily time limit on social media and interaction with devices. You'll decide just how much mental decluttering and uninterrupted face-to-face interaction you can stand— or stand to be without.

The metaphorical cord is in your hand. Go ahead. Pull the plug.

Moo

Driving along a country road, a child in the car notices cattle grazing in a pasture and excitedly announces: "Hey- herd of cows!" Invariably an adult responds: "Sure, I've heard of cows." (An old "dad joke" that has been delivered by me more often than I care to admit.)

Matters of animal husbandry aside, the presence of herd animals might also spur a self-reflective question that plumbs rather deeper than a dumb dad joke: *"How much of my own life is governed and lived like that of a herd animal? To what degree have I been dehumanized into some collective controlled by those who think it is appropriate for people to be herded?"*

Signs of human herding are all around us. Whenever we que in a line it's a tiny practice session for the herd life. If we follow the predefined promotion path of our employer rather than jumping to new employer, we practice a kind of herd obedience. When we submit to overreaching government edits concerning speech or personal behavior, we are surrendering our agency and simply mooing in harmony with the herd rather than thinking, speaking, and acting for ourselves. Small and large examples of herd conditioning and herd life are abundant.

Consider even the structural elements of city environments. Large numbers of people packed into spaces, stacked atop one another in skyscraping apartment buildings, and everywhere shuffled along in lines and conveyances. Wherever people are so densely packed strict regulation is put into place and so a herd is established.

Public transit systems are an obvious example. These systems are designed and run by city ranchers bent upon herding people like animals into public transit vehicles- the cattle cars of the human herd. This is not to say that public transit can't be a convenience, but convenient or not there is no denying its dehumanizing nature. One must que in line, then file into the cattle cars while mooing at others with every bump as you squeeze yourself tight for the ride only to filing out with the rest of the non-descript herd all headed to their corrals.

Everyday compliance with such herding may well impact our sense of autonomy and undermine our intrinsic motivation- key components in self-determination and overall psychological wellbeing. And when compliance with the herd also encompasses our ability to speak our

LIVE CONSCIOUSLY
Paying attention to the real VS Screen-numbed diversion

minds, dehumanization becomes complete, for individual thought and speech are the very stuff of humanity identity.

So, the next time someone in the car spots a herd of cows, consider the attendant existential question and any signs of dehumanization in your own life. Despite how placid the cow's existence may seem along the roadside, remember the inevitable fate of the members of a herd.

> *"It isn't what we say or think that defines us, but what we do."*
>
> Jane Austin

Indigestion

Just as it takes time to digest a meal, (some more than others), it also takes time to digest information. With both, the real value comes from the use of what was consumed, not simply in its storage.

Yet with so much plentiful food and information in the world we have a strong tendency to spend a great deal of our time consuming, but little time digesting and using what we've consumed.

So, our bodies store shapeless fat, and our minds store shapeless information. And we become rather shapeless in both regards.

Avoiding indigestion of both kinds is straightforward but takes conscious effort:

Consume, digest, and exercise to turn food into muscle and bone.

Consume, digest, and think to turn information into useful insight.

And don't be a pig on either count.

Time-share Contracts

When people sit in the same room together, each intently swiping through pages on the phone held closely to their face, they may absently believe that by virtue of their proximity they are somehow relating to each other, sharing time on the waves as we surf in a group, if you will. Yet, if they speak to each other at all, the interjected comments merely represent a small share of their attention, with all the

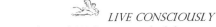

rest of their attention persistently directed at the small screen. The justification given is usually something like: *"I'm multi-tasking, but I AM paying attention. Besides, I'm just doing what we all do now."*

Sadly true.

"What we all do now" is, of course, the common practice of unconsciously but overtly displaying our lack of interest in the flesh-and-blood human being sitting directly across from us. Even pets get this silent treatment, sitting at their master's feet with an upturned face, craving attention from a person who is too absorbed by a tiny screen to notice. But unlike the master, they have no smart phone in which to bury their little face to distract from the dismissive treatment they are receiving from the one they love so unconditionally. Our human companions, by contrast, do have such a crutch at hand, in fact, in hand. And although the companions may ignore it, the dismissiveness that each person is exhibiting to the other is definite, profound, and deeply saddening.

A timeshare property is a place to which you are not sufficiently committed to purchase it outright. You just want to give it a little of your time. Likewise, are our timeshare relationships: the people who we, through our screen-absorbed actions, declare do not merit our full attention. They merit only a "share" that comes when there is a pause in the on-screen action.

Our timeshare friends and family feel this dismissal, or at least they would if they were not so busy unconsciously dismissing us too.

> *"Underneath this flabby exterior is an enormous lack of character."*
>
> Oscar Levant

Selfie-stuck

Social media is often used to build an exhaustive, if highly selective, public representation of oneself. These self-created worlds inevitably contain innumerable selfies to depict just how interesting, attractive, and admirable one is. Great care is taken to look just the right way while posing in just the right places such that the most excellent image of oneself is portrayed.

Perhaps this impulse is an unavoidable outgrowth of our sophisticated and handy personal media tools. Perhaps it reflects the powerful alure of the ever-expanding celebrity culture. Or perhaps it is merely a sign of neediness. Regardless, all that posing and photoshopping designed to create an idealized image of oneself does nothing to create a more ideal person. In fact, it may suppress efforts to create the real change that could have impact in real life. Which means that all the preening is really just a form of emotional masturbation.

Of course, everyone is entitled to a certain amount of bragging, and the sharing of experiences with others is a nice thing. But all those self-conscious selfies won't shape you into the person you're trying to depict online. They just steal the time you need to grow into that person and spend it to mask the limits of what you already are.

LIVE CONSCIOUSLY
Paying attention to the real VS Screen-numbed diversion

> *"There is no sun without shadow, and it is essential to know the night."*
>
> Albert Camus

The Price of Exhilaration

No one who lives in the monotonous sameness of some climes could understand the enchantment of an unexpected, lovely evening in a place where the weather is unpredictable; a place where the temperature is inconsistent and where the stars may be masked by clouds as often as not.

The appreciation and enjoyment of the unexpected, lovely evening in such places is sublime. I pity those who have unconsciously become inured to such delight through the persistent sameness of their moderate climate. The exhilarating joy in such moments comes only at the cost of many, less perfect moments. So much sweeter is this occasion.

Exhilaration in the human experience does not emerge from more of the same, however nice the same might be. It comes in the conscious experience of positive change.

Salted Caramel

If you have ever eaten a salted caramel, you know that the addition of the saltiness really brings out the delightful sweetness of the candy. The caramel would be delicious without the salt, but its addition creates a contrast that amplifies the experience.

Humans seem to gravitate toward contrasts like this. Perhaps this is because we so quickly grow accustomed to things and our familiarity

WHEN MONKEYS FLY

with them causes the delight that once came from those things to unconsciously diminish. Even our own accomplishments seldom provide long-lasting happiness. We quickly grow accustomed to the higher level we have achieved, then reflexively seek some new challenge to strive for a new feeling of accomplishment.

All of which is a good indicator that our perceptions are not absolute but, rather, are relative to our perception of other things. We measure by comparison, not on an objective scale. Thus, when things are going really well, we enjoy it for a time, then grow inured to that state and progressively become impatient, frustrated, and unhappy in our happiness.

The greyness of Dorothy's Kansas needed the contrast provided by the shocking colors of the Land of Oz to reset her perspective; the intense salt that made her conscious of the sweetness that was there all along.

LANDING

Live Consciously
Paying attention to the real vs Screen-numbed diversion

There is a thin line separating the depth of human life and the shallow existence of present-day Zombies. That line is the demarcation of a decision: whether to give in to the alure of popular shortcuts, trivial amusement, shallow thinking, comfort-seeking, and cursory connections. None of these Zombie-like behaviors reach deeply into the soul of real humanity.

The Tin Man was revered because he possessed the heart to deeply connect with his fellows on the journey. And while the heart may only be practical when it is made unbreakable, as the Wizard observed, both its joy and sorry can only be felt through consciousness. Otherwise, one lives the rusted life of a tin Zombie.

Consider the dehumanizing shortcuts that you see others taking. What ends do they typically yield? Rich human relationships and earned self-esteem, or isolation, shallowness, and disappointment? Despite the momentary hits of Dopamine that such shortcuts might produce, the cumulative effect is a steady slide into unconscious Zombiehood- the plodding life of one who is not really alive.

But if we avoid these lazy shortcuts, connecting authentically with our fellow humans face-to-face or shoulder-to-shoulder, and with ourselves too, we will never need to face the Zombie hoard. Because without our unconscious submission, the Zombies simply do not exist.

"Postmodernity is said to be a culture of fragmentary sensations, eclectic nostalgia, disposable simulacra, and promiscuous superficiality, in which the traditionally valued qualities of depth, coherence, meaning, originality, and authenticity are evacuated or dissolved amid the random swirl of empty signals."

Jean Baudrillard

LIVE CONSCIOUSLY
Paying attention to the real VS Screen-numbed diversion

WHEN MONKEYS FLY

Seek Meaning
Pursuit of purpose VS Lazy nihilism

Dorothy's adventure was a pursuit of the most central meaning in her young life- her love of the people in the place she so fondly called home. The girl assumed great challenges and dangers to return to that home, not so she could avail herself of the thrilling opportunities of Kansas, but to reconnect with that which held transcendent meaning for her.

But meaning is a complex and often controversial topic. People find meaning in many ways and ascribe its source variously. Some even emphatically reject the idea that life has any meaning at all beyond its material manifestation. So, rather than proselytizing for any active philosophy, in this flight we explore insights concerning the perception and pursuit of meaning. For without meaning our spirit can only devolve into the laziest of all philosophies: Nihilism.

WHEN MONKEYS FLY

A life lived without deep meaning cannot provide fulfillment. A life lived with meaningful purpose cannot help but deliver it. But what deep meaning there may be, must be discovered by each of us in our own way.

That can only happen if we first have the habit of looking for it.

SEEK MEANING
Pursuit of purpose VS Lazy nihilism

> "He who has a 'why' to live for can
> bear almost any 'how'."
>
> Friedrich Nietzsche

On Purpose

"I didn't do it on purpose," is the childhood explanation for a destructive act for which the child hopes to get a pass. Of course, even as adults we all sometimes commit actions that yield unintended results- results that did not serve our intended purpose. Which begs the broader question: What is your purpose and is what you are doing serving that purpose? In short: Are you doing the things you do on purpose, or just reflexively?

Only purpose can lead to fulfillment; the two are intrinsically intertwined. One doesn't find fulfillment without first having purpose, because without purpose we have nothing to fulfill. Fulfillment is the sense that your life counts for something valuable and that what you are doing is achieving that something.

Which means that mere happiness is not enough to fulfill your life. You might be quite happy sipping margaritas on the beach month after month, but it is quite unlikely that this will lead you to a place of fulfillment. Not to mention the sunburn! Ironically, the activities that do lead to fulfillment do not always elicit waves of happiness. Yet finding fulfillment always does make one happy in ways far deeper than merely lolling half buzzed in the sand. Fulfillment is the reward of a life lived with purpose.

So then, exactly what is purpose?

The John Templeton Foundation commissioned a review of the literature concerning the nature of human purpose, publishing an analysis which encompassed more than 120 publications covering a 60-year period. From this work a consensus definition for purpose emerged which proposed that: "Purpose is a stable and generalized intention to accomplish something that is at once personally meaningful and at the same time leads to productive engagement with some aspect of the world beyond the self."

That seems a good starting point for the virtuous cycle that can emerge from purposeful action: Set your sights on something that is both personally meaningful and also impacts the world outside yourself, unleash your curiosity to explore the purposeful actions you can take in the direction of your goal, then through striving toward that goal achieve the fulfillment and real happiness that results from living with purpose.

Don't get me wrong. Margaritas on the beach can be a very good thing. But it's not enough. Purpose is what gives life meaning and leads to the sublime happiness that only comes from fulfillment.

You want a life that is fulfilling, not merely time-filling. Whatever you do, you must do it with purpose.

SEEK MEANING
Pursuit of purpose VS Lazy nihilism

> *"Hell is a place where you have nothing to do but amuse yourself."*
>
> George Bernard Shaw

Arc of Life

Many think of the arc of life as moving through three phases of purpose:

1. Learn
2. Do
3. Teach

We spend the first third of life learning how to do things from those who have come before, the second third doing things by building on the accomplishments of the past to achieve new ones, and the last third passing along what we've learned and serving as the set of shoulders on which others stand.

That first phase we can do little about. But understanding the nature of the second and third phases offers some powerful purpose to be found within them. In his book: *From Strength to Strength,* Arthur Brooks cites the work of British-American psychologist Raymond Cattell who identified two types of intelligence that align neatly with those later two phases of life. Fluid Intelligence, the facility for invention and analysis is active during the "doing" phase, while Crystalized Intelligence, the facility for interpretation of ideas and for synthesis is active during the "teaching" phase, developing in strength just as Fluid Intelligence declines. Scientific support for an old adage.

This phased arc connects each generation to the next in a self-perpetuating circle of life driven by the meaningful purpose of each phase. It is an instructive model worthy of consideration by anyone in search of purpose or who is planning the next stage of life; assuming

WHEN MONKEYS FLY

that whatever it is that you learn-then-do-then-teach is something worthwhile.

But that's another matter.

SEEK MEANING
Pursuit of purpose VS Lazy nihilism

> *"Be yourself; everyone else is taken."*
> Oscar Wilde

Uniquely Meaningful

We are all members of groups- demographic groups, interest groups, social groups, political groups, professional groups, and the like. And while membership may have its privileges, being a group member is not, and should not be the defining characteristic and purpose of your life. You are much more than the groups to which you willingly belong or that you simply belong to by default.

You are a sovereign, self-aware, self-directing human being, not merely part of a system or collective, nor limited by someone's notion of your "identity". Your life is separate and distinct from all others regardless of shared characteristics, or interests, or beliefs. This is true because no one else has your particular combination of traits, history, experiences, talents, ambitions, tastes, ideas, and more. Far from being the replaceable part that identitarians would have you think you are, no other person can make the particular contributions that you can. And those contributions live on even after your death through the lives of those who you have influenced. Your uniqueness is not only a temporal reality, but also a transcendent one.

Given this uniqueness, surely your life has a unique purpose- something that only you can fulfill. Whatever that may be, it is the act of pursuing that purpose that can fill your life with meaning that is particular to you. Perhaps you find purpose through the development of products and services that others value and use, or perhaps it comes through charitable works, in creative endeavors, through research and discovery activities, by designing or building things, through the raising of children, or through any of myriad other possibilities. That unique purpose is your reason for being and is what gives your life a meaning that is yours alone.

The identitarians would prefer that you stay within the confines of the label they have in mind for you and will insist that you think and behave in ways they attribute to that label. They want only to assign you a role in pursuit of their purpose. Your unique purpose be damned.

Tell the identitarians to go to Hell. Live your purpose.

SEEK MEANING
Pursuit of purpose VS Lazy nihilism

> *"This virtue cannot be bestowed. It must be developed from within."*
>
> Frederick Douglass

A Stool to Stand On

We wouldn't think that a stool might represent great success. Surely the achievement of success would be better represented by a leather, executive office chair, a comfy lounge chair, or maybe a beach chair. But a stool?

Sit on whatever object you like- the stool is metaphorical because it is the legs that ultimately support your butt, and that's what this is about (the three legs, not your butt.)

Those legs represent the three core factors necessary if you are to achieve an unusually high level of success in any aspect of life. They are attributes found in every highly successful person, usually acquired through conscious, sustained effort over the course of years. They are each difficult to achieve, and each one builds upon the next. You can certainly attain just one or two and feel good about that. But outsized success requires all three:

Mastery *(Uncommon, world class skill)* Mastery is necessary to yield uncommon results. This is the phenomenal level of skill that Malcolm Gladwell was referring to in his book: *Outliers: The Story of Success* when he wrote about the need for 10,000 hours of practice to achieve mastery in a discipline.

Strength *(Tenaciousness, perseverance and will)* Without Strength, Mastery buckles when it hits its first obstacle. This is the trait of conscientiousness or what psychologist Angela Duckworth expressed as Grit: "perseverance and passion for long term goals."

WHEN MONKEYS FLY

Courage *(Willingness to assume real risks)* Without Courage, Mastery and Strength languish among the mundane, safe challenges that will never transport us to the highest level. That is- attaining an outsized level of success only comes from taking on outsized challenges. Outsized challenges present the very real possibility of outsized failures, so tackling those challenges despite the risk requires real courage.

You may notice that the three legs correspond well to the attributes of Dorothy's fellow travelers: Mastery= Brains; Strength= Heart[1]; Courage= Courage. Dorothy could not have attained her outsized success in the land of Oz if she did not have these characteristics at her disposal, personified by her companions.

But more than just enabling the outcomes we seek, valuing and fervently pursuing Mastery, Strength, and Courage shapes our character by building an uncommonly strong foundation to sit on.

Or better yet, to stand on.

SEEK MEANING
Pursuit of purpose VS Lazy nihilism

> *"Life is not a having and a getting, but a being and a becoming."*
>
> Myrna Loy

Keeping What You Give

The value of things we have is strongly influenced by what we gave to get them, whether measured by money, time, sacrifice, or other costs.

The acquisition of merchandise, money, award, position, or other tangible goals tends to be assigned value by the recipient in proportion to effort expended to acquire it. That is why when we work furiously to attain a difficult goal, we cherish the rewards tremendously. It is also why those who must struggle to gain even the most modest of things tend to appreciate those modest things greatly. They appreciate them in proportion to the effort given to get them. By contrast, people who have rather glorious things dropped into their laps through little or no effort of their own tend to appreciate those things very little. It is not ingratitude. It is just that the value of those things has been set low according to the low level of effort expended to get them.

Yes, a gift received without expending one's own effort can be greatly valued. But its value derives from the sentiment attached to the gift, and that value lasts only as long as the sentiment lasts. Which is why after a relationship break-up, formerly cherished gifts tend to go flying out the window. The formerly cherished gift takes on a new meaning that we don't appreciate.

While the things we gain easily may create excitement in the moment, there is little meaning to be found in the things themselves. It is our striving and effort that creates the value that really means something to us: the difficult challenge overcome, the goal attained, the struggle survived. It is our striving that bears the meaning.

Which is why it can be said that it's what you give that you get to keep.

Taking a Ride

While freedom in society offers the opportunity for pleasure-seeking, it becomes a moral hazard if you use it for nothing but pleasure-seeking.

Pleasure-seeking is just the holiday destination that freedom offers- nice for the occasional get-away. But freedom functions more powerfully when we are not on holiday. It lets you pave a road, mile-by-mile, to enriching destinations: to grow in ways that are important to you, to pursue your life goals and change those goals as you see fit, to love, to build, to speak your mind, and so much more. Far more than just offering the opportunity for careless time passing, freedom is the essential tool for all human flourishing.

Which means that freedom is really no holiday at all. If used only to pursue hedonistic pleasures, the greatest value of freedom is wasted: The freedom to live with meaningful purpose.

More succinctly stated by Matthew Arnold:

"Freedom is a very good horse to ride; but to ride somewhere."

SEEK MEANING
Pursuit of purpose VS Lazy nihilism

> *"The first gulp from the glass of natural sciences will turn you into an atheist, but at the bottom of the glass God is waiting for you."*
>
> Werner Heisenberg

The Atheist's Catch 22

The existence of God is often dismissed with the carelessly self-assured assertion that: "God is simply a construct created in a pre-modern world to explain the unexplained. But now we have science to do that."

But this attempt to leverage science to prove a negative violates a key tenant of the scientific method itself: always be open to further discovery. We know what we know today, but new discoveries may change that. Newtonian physics eventually admitted the deeper insights of Relativity, which later made room for Quantum Mechanics and later still began to embrace String Theory and then to question it. Each step revealed important and foundational insights, yet at no step did science broadcast a call to close our minds to the possibility of yet deeper insights that might follow, regardless of how preposterous such insights might seem at first.

It is profoundly unscientific to assert that a conception currently unsupported by evidence can be definitively and forever deemed impossible. That is to insist that what cannot be known today can never be; a declaration that there can never be further discovery and surprising insight into the conception. Just so, the pronouncement that "God does not exist" implicitly asserts that there can be no further discovery that might provide evidence of such existence. That assertion is not scientific proof. It's just a belief.

The Atheist's "scientific" declaration is a tacit claim that we possess the comprehensive knowledge of the universe necessary to support the declaration. But we are talking about a Universe that is comprised of

72.8% Dark Energy- something about which we know virtually nothing, 22.7% Dark Matter- another complete unknown, and just 4.5% Baryonic Matter- which is the stuff that comprises each of us and everything in the known universe. Just that 4.5% includes the 100 billion stars in our own galaxy as well as a hundred billion other galaxies beyond our own, each comprised of a hundred billion stars. And we're still only talking about the accessible three-dimensional Universe. Beyond that we postulate there exist several additional dimensions which, as three-dimensional creatures, we cannot even properly conceptualize as yet. Nor can we realistically fathom the real possibility that there exist an infinite number of additional Universes beyond all of this, perhaps existing simultaneously within the same space. And what of the foundational laws that govern even the sliver that we are aware of? Of these, we've so far merely scratched the surface.

Scientifically speaking, we know practically nothing of what there is. Which makes the hubris of a declaration about what "cannot" exist as vast as is the unknown. A lack of scientific proof for the God postulate can only offer the conclusion that no current evidence supports the existence of God. We simply don't have the data to make a definitive statement one way or the other. Moreover, to claim that one does possess the universal knowledge required make that definitive statement is to declare oneself to be the same omniscient God that is being denied- the Atheist's catch-22.

Here it is worth noting that in the debate concerning Quantum Mechanics during the early 20th century, Einstein famously rejected the theory with the quip: "God does not play dice." His foil in theoretical physics, Niels Bohr responded with the retort: "Einstein, stop telling God what to do." The key insight here is that despite the emphatic rejection of Quantum Mechanics by the greatest physicist of the time, science did not reject further discovery and discussion of the topic.

Clearly, belief in God is an act of faith. But so is belief in the non-existence of God because that viewpoint treads where science does not allow- closing the mind to possibility. It requires a leap of faith into the belief that what is presently known will never be contradicted. That is precisely the kind of closed-minded belief that science does not permit.

An alternative to either of these faithful stances on the existence of God, Agnosticism, does not stand on faith at all, but instead treads in a middle space that declares: "probably not." This would seem a more scientific response to the unknowable. Without explicit evidence for existence, "probably not" is a reasoned assessment that leaves itself open to further insights should they come.

Meanwhile, religious belief in God declaratively acknowledges itself to be an act of faith. It knowingly and transparently requires acceptance of what is unknowable and even of that which seems impossible. Afterall, faith is a decision to believe in what cannot be proven. That's what puts faith in God and faith in Atheism on a metaphysical par.

Yet, there is a key distinction between these two forms of faith. Religious faith aligns with the common human feeling that life has meaning beyond the purely physical and temporal world. Religious faith fulfills this gut instinct. By contrast, Atheistic faith dismisses this human feeling as a trick of the mind and leaves the gut feeling rather hollow.

Which leads us to consider the options of the Agnostic. He/she can remain straddling the fence between faiths, awaiting further enlightenment, or could simply take a leap of faith one way or the other- toward faith in God or faith in the absence of God. Either lets the Agnostic get off the fence to stand on ground that offers a more definitive way to approach life, albeit a faith-based way.

For one willing to take that leap, the operative question is: Which position of faith allows you to live in the more authentically human and meaningful way?

> *"The source of sorrows lies not in leaving life, but in leaving that which gives it meaning."*
>
> Raymond Radiguet

A Serene End

Many, when driven to contemplate their mortality, imagine a fantasy end featuring a satisfying crescendo or definitive closure for the loose ends of life, followed by a swift demise. But the typical reality of end-of-life differs significantly from this movie script finish.

We hang on to life as long as we can stand it, then continue hanging on even after we can't. This is human nature, or more likely, a primal element of animal nature. We hang on because there is always the promise of one more good day, or one more chance- *"if I can just make it to the next day."* It is an ennobling trait... the constant search for triumph over an unstoppable force.

But at some point in our inevitable demise, many become unable even to count the days nor to think of what could be in the next. For them, there exists only the moment and what the moment offers. And for them, without the context of what was or what lies ahead, this may be enough. It offers life just as it is- the only way that life really ever offers itself- one unknowable day at a time. Somehow, this simplicity seems to bring contentment to a few of those who find themselves living without the presence of mind to perceive their own context. Maybe it is only a shallow contentment, but perhaps it is a transcendent resolution.

I hope it might be the latter.

SEEK MEANING
Pursuit of purpose VS Lazy nihilism

A Dignified End

I recall the man at an assisted living facility for the elderly groaning and screaming out of the shear frustration of his life. *"I don't want to live like this!"*, he shouted desperately, followed by an angry and sarcastic: *"But they won't let you die... no they won't let you die!"* His utterances were issued as he rolled himself around a communal dining room, slumped in his wheelchair.

A group of elderly ladies who were rolled up to a nearby dining table were aghast. They were resigned to being pushed around on wheels, having a bib draped around their necks at meals, and being helped with toileting. His outburst was an insult to their placid resignation.

But a few people there still clung to the desire for something quite different, a death before the shadow of better times fades completely. A finish, not just a long, anguished, and demeaning fizzle into oblivion.

It comes down to timing. We want to hang on to life as long as we can stand it, but not a day longer. Yet the body or mind can turn the corner of no return in a day, leaving one who would wish for a different end incapable of taking a different path the very next day. And we never know when that "one day too long" may come.

So, it seems, there would have to be a willing sacrifice of some potentially good days to ensure that the line is not crossed into days we cannot stand. Perhaps for some there can be no serene resignation. And for them, perhaps life's meaning would be better suited by missing a last, little bit of good life than by suffering the last of one's life as a great deal of bad.

> "Once people stop believing in God, the problem is not that they will believe in nothing; rather, the problem is that they will believe anything."
>
> C.S. Lewis

The Material Lens

Secularists are not non-believers. In fact, many are great believers in gods of many kinds, akin to the ancient Greeks or Pagans who worshiped gods of sky, sea, crops, war, love, death, fertility, healing, and many more. Those idols were raised to explain mysteries, affirm assumptions, or to embody wishes. Serving similar purposes are the contemporary gods of secular belief. They codify presuppositions about the world and define virtue in ways that make it easily accessible, or at least claimable. But the codifiers look only through a materialist lens. They are able only to apprehend a three-dimensional, material world, and so the virtue they define is limited by the material.

These materialist gods of our contemporary world are many: the god of equity; the god of safety; the god of climate; the god of justice; the gods of identities; the god of science; the god of government; the god of self-esteem; the god of celebrity; the god of ego; and many others- a panoply of gods to worship in the absence of God. A return to the ancient way.

All these gods purport to inject meaning into the lives of believers yet, at best, they offer solutions only to material problems. And like the sacrifices made to ancient gods, the believer's offerings are often unproductive or even counterproductive in the long run. Moreover, they never offer a vision that unifies the physical with the metaphysical, nor speak to the deepest part of human experience- that which transcends the merely material.

SEEK MEANING
Pursuit of purpose VS Lazy nihilism

Yet, like the gods of the ancients, questioning the wisdom of belief in these gods is considered heresy and treated with extreme prejudice by secular religious zealots. Like the ancients, their beliefs are as rigid as their god's foundations are flimsy.

So, while these various gods may have meaningful purposes when focused through the three-dimensional lens of the material, they fail to offer the transcendent meaning that embraces eternal values of truth, rightness, and beauty. Seeing farther and more deeply requires a lens of another kind, and a mind probing and open enough to look through it.

LANDING

Seek Meaning
Pursuit of purpose vs Lazy nihilism

Life is complex and difficult enough to occupy all your time pursuing tangible and useful goals and with the enjoyment of pleasures. But there is more than just that for you.

The fact that you are a sovereign and unique human being implies that there is unique meaning to your existence. It implies that your life is more than just the day-by-day survival and temporal occupations of a creature trudging along toward death. Or, at least, it should be more than that. Contemplating the millennia of accumulated human experience, religious and philosophical teachings, and the events of our own lives offer clues as to the meaning of it all, though we can never know for sure. Yet, meaning would be the point- the reason for being which we can strive to fulfill. It is the striving toward such fulfillment that makes this difficult and exhilarating journey worth the effort and, maybe, what drives us to hang on even after life becomes unbearable. A sovereign meaning, perhaps vague and elusive, but one which lets us persist despite pain or emptiness or despair, never quite attaining our target, but never failing to try.

Over the rainbow resided a little girl's simple meaning- the family and friends that gave purpose to her striving. But as unique, sovereign beings the search for purposeful meaning can be vexing: "Why am I here? What am I to do? What purpose must I fulfill?" Yet the comprehensive revelation that would answer all such questions will never come. So, we must grab the fragments of meaning that emerge from time to time- the deep insights that coalesce in our unique minds and the deep fulfillments that sometimes flood our unique hearts, to

SEEK MEANING
Pursuit of purpose VS Lazy nihilism

courageously connect these dots along the path to form a picture of our unique meaning.

Before the end of life, we must each resolve just what it all means lest we vanish into a question mark- the unfinished statement of a life. So, despite the never finished nature of our understanding, we must decide on the meaningful purpose of our life well before the end comes, while still there is time to live that purpose, not just to die with it.

The life lived without deep meaning cannot provide fulfillment. The life lived with meaningful purpose cannot help but deliver it.

> *"The question is not to know what is the meaning of life, but what meaning I can give to my life."*
>
> *Dalai Lama*

WHEN MONKEYS FLY

Embrace Adversity
Growing through challenge VS Learned helplessness

Though not without fear, Dorothy embraced the adversity of her adventure in the land of Oz, replete with its surprises, threats, and terrors. Her companions too embraced their hardships and deficiencies with a resolve to overcome the adversity they faced, be it lack of brains, or heart, or even courage.

But our foolish world seems to teach helplessness rather than perseverance.

In this flight we'll examine the impulse of those who tend to surrender to adversity and the attitudes and actions that lead to overcoming obstacles instead.

Consider the dog that, through some terrible accident, finds it has just three legs left. Neither the dog nor any living thing can control all accidents and circumstances of life. But we can control how we think about those circumstances and what we do about them. Even the three-legged dog can choose its response to a bad situation, i.e.: to whimper in the corner or learn to run in a new way.

Such strength of character stems from the habit of embracing adversities rather than sulking. That uncomfortable embrace makes it possible to reshape adversity from a lesson about helplessness into a dynamic challenge that drives us to become more.

> *"The purpose of pain is not so much to punish your actions as it is to prepare you for a better future."*

Whine Glasses

It matters less how full the glass is than what it contains. The spritzer recipe used by the happiest of life's mixologists calls for a full measure of solution and just a dash of whine. Yet, most of us reverse this recipe by including just a dribble of solution but a heaping portion of whine.

The high-whine blend is particularly addictive because each self-absorbed drink of it seems to taste better than the last. Keep it up and pretty soon you've got a drinking problem, though one without the usual, temporary carefree feeling. This drinking problem is all downside, serving only to prolong the very hurt you were trying to appease in a never-ending hangover of self-pity.

Alas, there is no AA for whiners, so it's vital to self-regulate and assure that your glass never contains more than a splash of the stuff. Embracing, rather than complaining about adversity, leaves room for plenty of solutioning which, in turn, creates new space for all the other wonderous stuff of life that you may then imbibe. It lets you take on life with the mixologist's talent for making a delightful concoction from unlikely ingredients, while others gloomily gargle whine.

Keep the cocktail mixture in its proper balance. Shaken or stirred is your choice. Either way, cutting back on the whine will save you, (and those around you), from a life filled with pounding hangovers.

> "We all get into trouble. It's how we
> get out of it that counts."
>
> Unknown

Losing Winners

Handing out participation trophies does not make everyone a winner any more than great singers are created by telling everyone at Karaoke night that they sounded "fantastic."

In the race, little Johnny came in near the back of the pack, but the participation trophy that he and everyone else were given is supposed to protect his self-esteem from this reality. Johnny may not be fast, but he isn't stupid. He knows what happened. Yet the participation trophy actually celebrates what he knows to be a poor performance and tacitly communicates to Johnny that there is little reason to improve.

High achievement becomes a sucker's quest when there is little or no extra reward for working really hard to achieve at a high level. Absent high-level reward, the better performers see little reason to put in that high-level effort. Meantime, Johnny can't see why he should struggle to lift his performance since he gains similar benefit without the effort, and everyone seems so proud of him just where he is. When the winning/losing dichotomy is missing, average performance declines as losers fail to improve and winners lose their drive. So, while the notion is to make everyone a winner, in fact, everyone ends up a loser despite declared victory.

Contrast this to a less contrived approach where failure is allowed to be recognized as failure and is left unrewarded. Despite its sting, or perhaps because of it, the hard lesson serves to fuel a desire to do better and motivates the changes and effort needed to advance. If we examine the history of virtually any celebrated winner, we find a path littered with key adversities, disappointments, and losses. We never find winners who have also not been losers. But they never celebrated

EMBRACE ADVERSITY
Growing through challenge VS Learned helplessness

their losses. They sweated those losses, embracing the challenge presented by the loss, driving them to strive for better.

True caring about people requires that we acknowledge their failures so that they can learn the tough lessons of loss, then make changes for their own betterment. Yes, your impulse is to protect those who are precious to you from the despair of losing. But doing so only stunts their growth, trading long-term success for some short-term cold comfort.

Take away the adversity of losing and the path to success is missing a crucial step.

Ultimately, we lose potential winners.

> *"Real courage is when you know you're licked before you begin, but you begin anyway and see it through."*

Harper Lee

Batter Up

In baseball, the best in the world fail 2 out of 3 times at bat. Yet, despite failing most of the time, they are acclaimed for their excellence.

Some might be inclined to say: *"Well, this sport is obviously too hard then... we should make the game easier so more people can succeed!"* But this misses the very human point of the game. It is the difficulty that makes the game both exciting to watch and rewarding to play. We thrill when competitors show the heart and courage to take on challenge when it is difficult or, in fact, expressly because it is difficult.

Life is pretty challenging too, so we all fail an awful lot. Fortunately, unlike the game, in life we're not done after 3 strikes nor even 3 outs. We can have as many at-bats as we are willing to step-up and take. But that means that you've got to be willing to step-up despite knowing that when you do your effort may only yield yet another swing-and-a-miss.

Swing away, because in the end it is those who take a lot of at-bats who end up with the most hits, despite all the strikes and outs. While we are all sure to fail quite a lot in our various endeavors, if you have heart enough to embrace that adversity and keep going, you'll end up getting a lot of hits.

You're at the plate every day. Swing away.

EMBRACE ADVERSITY
Growing through challenge VS Learned helplessness

> *"He that struggles with us strengthens our nerves, and sharpens our skill. Our antagonist is our helper."*
>
> Edmund Burke

Unsafe Spaces

If you have anxieties or insecurities, (who doesn't?), you can take a lesson from Dorothy's fellow travelers: Expose yourself to the things that you fear rather than forever avoiding those things. The Lion had lived in fear of even the faintest threats, but after joining Dorothy's band of travelers he was exposed to danger after danger, ultimately finding his inner courage when compelled to face the Witch and her guards on Dorothy's behalf.

The longer we evade the things that frighten us the more we prolong and cement their power over us. It takes repeated exposure to the adversities that frighten you to build a psychological immune system that can defeat those fears through forward movement. This is the foundation of the well-accepted Exposure Therapy technique used in psychological practice. The American Psychological Association states that this technique: "has been scientifically demonstrated to be a helpful treatment or treatment component for a range of problems, including: Phobias; Panic Disorder; Social Anxiety Disorder; Obsessive-Compulsive Disorder; Posttraumatic Stress Disorder; and Generalized Anxiety Disorder." Fear of witches is not explicitly mentioned but would seem to fit the description.

Yet a complete cure from fear need not be the goal in any case. Ultimately, Lion learned that courage is not the lack of fear, it is the willingness to move forward despite one's fear. This mindset is often described by combat veterans and first responders, indicating that in dangerous, life-threatening situations they do indeed feel fear but do not allow it to paralyze them. Over time, continued exposure to such fearful situations gradually diminishes anxiety, making it ever easier to move toward the sound of gunfire rather than to run away. But the fear never vanishes completely. It is primarily one's response to fear that changes.

Victory over fear comes only by embracing your journey into the unsafe spaces where fears reside. Challenge your fears and you may find not only that what you feared was not so fearsome after all, but that you are able to move forward through that fear to accomplish what you set out to do despite it.

> "There can be no independence without a large share of self-dependence"
>
> Frederic Douglas

Prepare for Courage

Safety is an impossible goal. There are always dangers lurking, or at minimum there are obstacles that at first appear to be dangers.

Since dangers cannot forever be avoided, you must prepare to meet their challenge. Ready yourself by developing the necessary skills and attitudes that will let you tackle them with aplomb. When prepared, the dangers look a little less dangerous and courage comes more easily.

There is no safety. Prepare for what may come, and courage surely will.

> *"There is nothing noble in being superior to your fellow men. True nobility lies in being superior to your former self."*
>
> Ernest Hemmingway

More of You

There are many kinds of discomfort, ranging from the unpleasant discomfort of eating too much to the invigorating discomfort of pushing your abilities to the limits. Fulfillment doesn't come from the first, unless that third time through the buffet line fulfills some odd, life ambition. But fulfillment does come from the second kind when we stretch the limits of our capabilities beyond our discomfort threshold to find the higher level we never thought we possessed. With each threshold passed, we build strength (physical, mental, emotional), and so set the new discomfort threshold a bit higher than the last.

The difficulty we face in accepting discomfort (of the right kind) is that we tend to prioritize happiness over fulfillment. But while happiness is nice, it is evanescent. By contrast, fulfillment is deep and persistent. Yet the process of pursuing fulfillment is not always a happy and comfortable journey. So, we often avoid paths to fulfillment to keep ourselves happy in the moment, even though we end up suffering the unhappy consequences of those actions. Comfort eating makes us fat. Avoiding stressful situations only increases our discomfort with stress. Happily occupying our mind with banal, unchallenging entertainment makes us dull. None of these kinds of things are fulfilling. So, the irony of the pursuit of happiness is that by consistently prioritizing current happiness you may never reach the long-term happiness of fulfillment because you've forever avoided the unhappy places that necessarily fall along the way.

Success, according to whatever vision of success you have, requires that you seek out that which is uncomfortable and embrace discomfort as your friend. This new friend is not the sweet type who is dedicated

 *EMBRACE ADVERSITY*
Growing through challenge VS Learned helplessness

simply to making you feel happy and comfortable. This is the resolute friend who cares enough to test your limits so you can attain something far, far greater than mere comfort: fulfillment.

That discomforting friend understands that doing what is uncomfortable makes you more while, like that third trip through the buffet line, doing what is comfortable just makes more of you.

> *"Diligence is the mother of good luck."*
>
> Benjamin Franklin

Getting There

There is no such thing as: *"You can't get there from here,"* despite the proclamation of the proverbial, rural gas station attendant when asked for directions.

If you really, really want to get somewhere- there is always a way. That way may present much adversity. It may be circuitous and plodding, or long and exhausting, or ferociously difficult. It may require the taking of tiny, incremental steps, or backtracking a hundred miles, or sacrificing in the near term, or even refining your notion of the appropriate destination.

The question is not: "Do I know the way?", but rather: "How can I embrace the difficulties, whatever they may be, while finding a way?"

Well-meaning gas station attendants notwithstanding, you can get there from here.

EMBRACE ADVERSITY
Growing through challenge VS Learned helplessness

> *"If you would only recognize that life is hard, things would be so much easier for you."*
>
> Louis D. Brandeis

Too Hard Not To

Everything that is worthwhile is hard: Love is hard, staying in shape is hard, tolerance is hard, learning is hard, patience is hard, building the new and rebuilding the broken is hard, relationships are hard, change is hard, even freedom is hard. Add your own items to the list. All the really good stuff of life is hard because what is truly good doesn't come easily. You must work at it all.

When you look back at the things you have done, be alarmed if your assessment highlights how easy it all was. That's a signal that you haven't honestly pursued all the really good things of life that just aren't so easy. Instead, you want your assessment of the journey traveled to sound something like: "My God, that was so very hard... but it was worth it."

Even the ordinary activities of daily life conjure up plenty of unexpected hard challenges to deal with, just to get by. These can seem intolerable because the meeting of mundane challenges yields only mundane rewards. To rise above the mundane, you must take on the kind of big challenges that can lead to exciting and fulfilling results. That's harder still. But life is just too hard to bear without the exhilarating results of having done well what is really, really hard.

Inspired by the wisdom of Jordon Peterson

> *"I have always found that plans are useless,
> but planning is indispensable."*
>
> Dwight D. Eisenhower

Pivot to Success

Most successes in life stem from a pivot, not the original plan. The pivot happens after the journey has already started, is spurred by a new discovery or obstacle, and offers a better alternative that must be quickly adopted to adapt to, or capitalize upon, the new circumstances. Successes so often stem from a pivot because plans can offer only a starting point, while pivots are a response to actual experiences.

This is no excuse for failing to plan. In fact, your initial planning around any goal is essential to being ready for the pivot that you cannot see coming. That advance planning establishes your base understanding of the world through which you must navigate- an understanding necessary for the quick formulation of the pivot that adapts to changing circumstances.

But it takes brutal honesty to admit when your original plan will no longer take you where originally desired. Many will flog a plan that has outlived circumstances. Better to simply embrace the hard lesson of the failing plan so you can then devise the pivot that will yield better results.

More likely than not, the pivot you didn't count on is the very change of plan that will lead to the success that you did.

EMBRACE ADVERSITY
Growing through challenge VS Learned helplessness

> *"Those are my principles, and if you don't like them... well, I have others."*
>
> Groucho Marx

Leading Attributes

Regardless of what level of formal leadership you have gained, you can always lead in informal, yet vital ways.

You can lead by example of your heart and determination, your integrity, your compassion, your energy, your courage, your positive attitude, your relentless effort, your grace under pressure, your kindness, your fairness, your passion, your trustworthiness, your strength, and through a dozen other attributes that others admire and look up to.

While these demonstrations of character may not carry official authority, they are nevertheless potent kinds of leadership. The people around you are each facing adversities for which they could use some guidance. They can follow your lead when you exhibit such admirable qualities consistently. They can embrace the example you set and feel inspired to embody those characteristics in themselves. In the process, you lead them in essential and potentially life-changing ways that help them to embrace and deal with the various adversities they face.

You can be a leader even if you don't have the title that would signify it, just so long as you exhibit attributes that are worth following.

LANDING

Embrace Adversity
Growing through challenge VS Learned helplessness

The three-legged dog does not pity himself. He plays, and runs, and wags his tail in delight at the sight of other dogs and of his owner. Thoughts of his difficulties, his injuries, the injustice of it all... these things do not enter his mind. He lives his life with exuberance.

By contrast, the self-pity we too often indulge destroys everything in its wake- our joy, our motivation, our relationships, our very character... leaving nothing of our life but a whimper. But to live in that way is not fate. It is a decision. Psychiatrist and Holocaust survivor Viktor Frankl put it this way: "Forces beyond your control can take away everything you possess except one thing, your freedom to choose how you will respond to the situation."

We are all wounded, and like Dorothy, sometimes we are lost and confused. But you need not let your wounds cripple your spirit. Instead, you can embrace the adversities that have befallen you, learn from them, and adapt. You can take count of the million blessings that you still have and celebrate that wealth. You can take control of how you react and, instead of despairing, conceive an exciting vision of the new, fulfilling destinations that you will now pursue with exuberance.

Live with the unencumbered clarity of the three-legged dog.

EMBRACE ADVERSITY
Growing through challenge VS Learned helplessness

> *"The world breaks everyone,
> and afterward, some are strong
> at the broken places."*
>
> Ernest Hemmingway

WHEN MONKEYS FLY

Epilogue

Dorothy's journey ultimately led her back to her beginnings, as in the often-quoted lines from the TS Eliot poem *Little Gidding*:

> "And the end of all our exploring
> Will be to arrive where we started
> And know the place for the first time.
> Through the unknown, remembered gate
> When the last of earth left to discover
> Is that which was the beginning;
> At the source of the longest river"

Wisdom is, indeed, a very, very long river, carved through the banks of time over countless generations of human experience. Yet, Dorothy traversed several of its lessons in the course of just one sleep.

Several kinds of thinking and actions described and analogized herein may be deemed wise because those things tend to lead to better ends. Explications of comparatively foolish notions describe thinking and actions that tend to achieve the opposite. Whatever the mechanism by which wisdom operates, whether grounded in the cognitive sciences, real-life processes, or the transcendent, better ends would be the point of wisdom.

Of course, each person will have their own perspective on these insights. You might feel outraged by what you perceive to be the heresy of some of these ideas. By contrast, perhaps you feel uplifted by new or renewed conceptions- an unknown, remembered gate. Yet, regardless of how you view the book's various discernments, if you are now thinking about how to expand the wisdom that might guide your life to better ends, the monkeys have done their work.

But exercising wisdom in our foolish age can feel like sailing against the wind. The media types, politicians, and activists constantly spin-up cyclones of blustering opinion, vaporous policies, and airy notions of every kind. We're bound to be swept up into at least some of these tornadic thought bubbles. Which is why the flying monkeys come equipped with a pin. Now the pin is in your hand, poised to prick whatever foolish thought bubbles may have engulfed you (be they social, political, emotional, or other).

Those churning thought bubbles are formed from one-part orthodoxy and two-parts conformity. Unquestioned orthodoxy comprises the containing shape of the bubble. The reflections we see from inside, of ourselves and fellow captives, are the self-reinforcement mechanism that holds us in group think conformance. Like the Stockholm Syndrome victim, you may believe that the whirling notions that now contain you are enlightened and noble. If they are, your probing reassessment will only confirm that. But if mere questioning can pop the bubble, perhaps its notions are not so wise after all. Perhaps you would be best served by being free of its foolishness so you may embrace some wiser habits.

Consider a future in which you do a better job of always speaking your mind even when the opposition seems stacked against you; rejecting enticing comforts if they impede the freedom needed to pursue your best self; taking responsibility even when an excuse is at hand; exercising careful skepticism in pursuit of truth; rejecting nonsense even when nonsense is in fashion; putting aside the naïve notions that left you gullible for too long; valuing people for who, not what they are; avoiding distractions to have a fully human experience of life;

abandoning lazy materialism to bolster your spirit instead; and embracing hardship so it may empower, not disempower you.

These are not the only wise habits of course, but they are good companions for your journey and, perhaps, a motivation to seek further wisdom available in great literature, philosophical works, psychological insights, religious teachings, and people with greater and different experience than yourself. Wise habits help to keep us on the road by connecting the dots of our experience to more clearly perceive where the road leads, and thus, which turns will be wise, or not.

Like Dorothy, your exploring may ultimately lead to your beginnings and, perhaps, to know the wisdom of the place for the first time. Old wisdom tends to be the best kind- "the source of the longest river." Regardless of your direction of travel, the churning, mind clouds of foolishness that spin up along the way can be popped by the keen point of wise thinking. Moreover, with each bubble burst not only is your own mind freed, but your behavior also encourages others to adopt some wise habits themselves.

With or without the help of a squadron of wise, aerial simians.

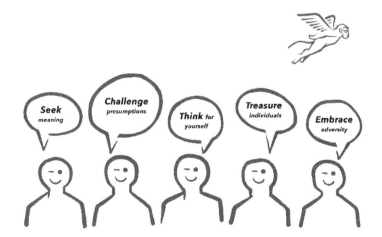

WHEN MONKEYS FLY

BAGGAGE CLAIM

A Monkey Made Me Do It

This book began as a collection of cryptic thoughts thumbed out on my phone at odd hours of the night whenever an idea would occur to me or when I ran across one that I thought was profound. I let these missives collect in my in-box for a couple years before I began reading through them and, subsequently, began to believe that there might be something there that would be useful to others- not just a rough record of my thoughts. So, I started to clean them up, rewriting repeatedly to flush out each insight. Clearly the monkey was on my back, and as I continued, I was encouraged in my aspiration.

However, progressively I came to see how much of what I had recorded was little more than snarky remarks on the beliefs or behaviors of those with whom I found disagreement. The more I clarified those thoughts, the more I realized that many of my missives were just me ranting to me- not something that would speak to anyone who thought outside the bubble of my own opinions. I also saw how captive I was within my own bubble of thought. That was terrifically disheartening.

But it was also a key insight. Namely: that we all live within a bubble of thoughts and opinions, and that our inability to embrace or even to hear ideas outside our own sphere was, perhaps, the source of the polarization between people that now seems so pervasive. So, I purged the snarky commentary as best I could, focusing instead on perspectives that might prompt insights or start a dialog.

That effort turned out to be terrifically difficult. It's hard to pierce your own thought bubble or the swirling bluster of the world to express ideas objectively and in a way that might connect with others. It's harder still to crystallize wisdom. I don't know how successful my effort was, but this collection is the result of trying.

Bill Haines

Flying Monkeys?

The term is a reference to the winged monkeys employed by the Wicked Witch of the West character in Frank Baum's children's book: *The Wonderful Wizard of Oz*, popularized by the 1939 film: *The Wizard of Oz*. The term has more recently been adopted in popular psychology to describe people who, in some way, do the bidding of a narcissist in order to damage his/her foes. Such flying monkeys are much in evidence in our foolish world.

In the original book's tale, however, after having served the Witch of the West the monkeys served Dorothy instead, flying her little troop over impassable land barriers to reach their final, happy destinations. Later the flying monkeys were given freedom by the good witch Glinda such that they were no longer obligated to serve anyone. It is those free flying monkeys that are the namesake of this book. Their mischief is unleased only against our own narcissistic tendency to sleepily loll within the overinflated thought bubbles that cause us to ignore the wisdom all around us.

Footnote

[1] In the book *The Wonderful Wizard of Oz* the back story of the Tin Man explains how, when he was a woodsman, he had planned to marry a Munchkin girl who served the Wicked Witch. But the Wicked Witch wanted the girl to remain in her service, so she put a spell on the Woodsman that caused him to chop off his own body parts, one by one. Each time the Woodsman would sever a limb he would visit a tin smith and have him create a tin replacement until, finally, he was completely made of tin- a Tin Man. Despite all of this, the Tin Man exhibited the Strength to continue toward his goal of marrying the Munchkin girl. His brand of heart was not only sensitive, it was strong.

From the Author

I'm a blissfully married man, father of three, business advisor, author, frequent swinger of hammers, occasional drinker of good whisky, and one who is forever agitated by people who won't think for themselves long enough to see the obvious.

How does that, in any way, qualify me to write about wisdom? Obviously, I'm not the arbiter of eternal wisdom, I'm merely a consumer of it. But, like many, life's experiences have pointed to a particular way of thinking about wisdom. Losing my father at a young age drove home the concept of necessity and its constant companion, pragmatism. My long career in business as an executive and later as an advisor taught the same core lesson though in differently tangible terms. Then too, the various hard knocks of life do a wonderful job of punctuating this notion for us all.

My takeaway is that necessity may be the most powerful agent for distilling the essential truths that govern things. Spend enough time focused on pragmatic necessity and the difference between things that are wise and those that are not becomes plain. That is- if you burst the swirling bubbles of presupposition and think long term.

Then too, living in a place not far from Dorothy's Kansas, that pragmatic mindset is a kind of cultural standard and was bound to highlight the abundance of unwise thinking churning its way through the rest of the country and the world. The perspective is different here in the heartland of America and I suspect that wisdom is sustained more easily here than in some of its extremities. It is a centering kind of place.

In any case, I'm not one who binges on social media, nor advocates in politics, nor prescribes to causes du jour. None of that seems very wise to me. Anyway, wisdom is a journey, not an argument. So, my goal for

When Monkeys Fly was not so much to express wisdom as it was to highlight the brand of thinking that can keep you on the road to wisdom and to question the synthetic notions that will lead you astray.

… At least for those willing to think for themselves long enough to see what seems obvious to we necessity-based pragmatists.

Attribution

Where known, quotes are attributed to their authors as best I could determine. Some are paraphrased, and I apologize for any errors of interpretation that I may have injected in the process. Some essays are noted to have been inspired by the work of others and are therefore subject to the same errors of interpretation, and again, I apologize for any errors that I have made. Finally, quotes that are unattributed are my own- or at least I think they are. I acknowledge that I might well have come across some of these in the past and that they may have rattled around in my head for enough years that I came to think of them as my own. Once again, I apologize for any such error I may have committed.

Thanks

Thanks to all the free-flying minds whose work inspired. Thanks also to Rich Murphy and team for work on the book's graphics, to all those who offered encouragement, endured tedious review of this book, and who tolerated me and my monkeys along the way.

Author's Quotes

To the best of my knowledge the following is a list of my own statements. That is not to say that all the ideas expressed are purely original. In fact, it is likely that many of these ideas have been previously expressed by others in different and perhaps better words. It's also quite possible that some belong, verbatim, to someone else, and merely the case that I've lived with those potent words in my head for so long that I came to believe they were my own. If such is the case for any of these unattributed quotes, I apologize and would welcome correction.

Of course, the book also contains many attributed quotes which are pure gems (see: *Notable Epigrams*). Still, I hope that a few of my own might offer some merit too- but you are the judge. So, bearing in mind the above disclaimer, and at the distinct risk of having my bubble burst by the reader, here is a compilation of what I believe are original quotes from the book that you might enjoy:

Think and Speak for Yourself

"Things don't advance much when the Medieval impulse prevails because it's terrifically difficult to have a reasoned discussion while being drawn and quartered."

"Agree to be disagreeable."

"This notion that speech is "dangerous" signals the Orwellian start of a decent into a modern, Medieval dungeon of the mind, reducing the range of allowable thought to a mere blend of chimerical edicts and angry mob rule. Violence inevitably follows such a descent. It always has."

"Place limits upon the hurling of opinions and the rocks start flying again."

WHEN MONKEYS FLY

"A person's thinking and ideas do not, and should not be expected to, neatly align with that person's demographic characteristics."

"It takes only a little imagination to come up with a way to commit suicide. But it takes a lack of imagination to commit intellectual suicide."

"When parties remain at loggerheads, unwilling to engage, their thinking stales and dies in a kind of intellectual suicide pact."

"If you don't think and speak for yourself, you are just another set of arms and legs for someone else's mind."

Choose Freedom Over Comfort

"Equality of outcome always devolves into equality of misery."

"Pay close attention to the person standing behind the curtain of pretty promises."

"What is free in one place exacts a cost in another. 'Free' is a zero-sum game."

"If your view of opportunity is that of a fixed pie, the argument is about who gets what size slice. But if your view of opportunity is that of a bigger pie, the relative size of the slices matters far less than does the overall size of the growing pie."

"If you are not acquainted with the term 'useful idiot', you are likely on the way to becoming one."

"If the stark lessons of the 20th century have taught us nothing else, they have taught us that Caring and Fairness cannot prevail without the safety mechanism of Liberty."

Own Your Outcomes

"Don't just honk. Do something."

"Don't rage at the wind. Make use of it. Tack."

"Patience is a great virtue… if you have time for that sort of thing."

"Kill the monster while it's small."

"When we pursue one elevated goal, they all get closer."

"Weed the garden of your mind to remove thoughts that will tend to lead you astray and choke the roots of your best opportunities."

"You can learn from the past, but you can't tidy it up."

"Beware ease."

"The bill for inaction comes only after the fact, like that of the meal ordered from a menu without prices printed on it. You ordered this meal in ignorance by failing to ask the price. Now that you've eaten, it's too late. The check will come."

"There are no perfect moments. Take action when the next good one comes along or you'll be stuck forever awaiting the perfect moment."

"When a relatively comfortable safety net is persistently and unconditionally available, people don't work too hard to keep from falling."

"You have the same 24 hours as everyone else. That's all there is. How will you use yours?"

"If you can't bite, or can't bring yourself to do so, you will usually be bitten."

WHEN MONKEYS FLY

Be Skeptical

"In business there is competition. In policymaking there is argumentation. Competition tends to expose the truth. Argumentation tends to obfuscate it."

"View certainty with skepticism."

"Good intentions do not necessarily make for good policy."

"It need not be a dystopian future if we can reject the animal impulse to tear-down and muster the noble will to build-up instead."

"If we do not openly discuss our moral differences, we are doomed to bloody battle over them."

"Ask uncomfortable questions."

Confront Fashionable Nonsense

"At its essence, Postmodernism is just a fancy way of believing in nothing."

"It should make us all feel uncomfortable when someone refuses to hear an opposing point of view."

"No past life can escape the shallow judgement of those without historical perspective."

"It is fair to hate certain ideas, but unfair to hate the people who hold those ideas."

"Acquiescence to the idea that words mean things that they never have, that history can be taken out of context, and that time-tested principles must be abolished, is to stare into the bright lights of the Inquisitor and declare: "I see 5"."

Put Away Childish Things

"We must all shed the naïve belief that the world should be perfect and, instead, get good at dealing with the perfect messes it regularly puts before us."

"Mature people have a high level of concern for the wellbeing of others, but relatively low concern for transitory emotions. The immature have the opposite concerns."

"Maturity comes only when the desire to grow overcomes the desire to fit in."

"To be mature is to think for yourself."

"Love of theory actively destroys something real that might have been."

"It's hard to imagine anyone so ill equipped to offer real-world insight or perspective than actors, nor anyone who's apparent earnestness could be more misleading."

"When it comes to wisdom, old is good."

"Wisdom requires humility."

"Western civilization is the worst civilization in the world- except for all the others."

"The water of adult life feels cold at first, but it's no good just dipping your toes in occasionally then running away from the water's edge. Dive in, headfirst."

"The future does not belong to the children. It belongs to children who become grown-ups."

WHEN MONKEYS FLY

Treasure Individuals

"When we begin to treat people as individual human beings rather than as cattle of one herd or another, we contribute to the dignity of all. Including our own dignity."

"Assuming that an individual has the characteristics of his group is both a factual error and a moral one."

"The mouth is a two-way portal: What goes in determines how healthy your body can be. What comes out determines how healthy your relationships can be."

"Most people would be both thinner and appear less vapid if they just kept their mouths closed more of the time."

"Educate rather than demean. Encourage rather than chastise. Enjoy rather than resent."

"When you do what is good for you rather than what is bad, you benefit not only yourself but also those who love you. You help them to achieve the best outcomes for something that is dear to them: You."

"You most certainly may embrace your politics with great passion. But you must love your friends and family with even greater passion."

"Incessantly saying "I love you" is not love. Doing the grocery shopping when it's not your turn is love."

"Love without friendship is impractical and stifling. Friendship without romantic love is just, well, friendship. You need both to make a marriage work."

"As much as we are told that "love conquers all", turns out that it doesn't conquer the day-to-day friction that results when two people try to cooperate over the chores."

"The unnecessary nature of an unnecessary act of service is what makes it so necessarily meaningful."

"Be strong, but kind. Be kind, but strong."

Live Consciously
"The exhilarating delight in some moments comes only at the cost of many, less perfect moments. So much the sweeter is this occasion."

"Screens are often used merely as chewing gum for the mind"

"Like the body, your character requires consistent, healthy nourishment."

"In the same way we sometimes need to reset the router in order to get a good connection, we should occasionally disconnect from that big stream of outside data so we can reset our connection with the actual humans of our physical world."

"With a perception of things that is drawn principally from communications that only delve skin deep, your thoughts remain a superficial scab, easily peeled away by the next scratch."

"The measure of our delight is not in the measure of the thing or the event- it lies in its contrast to something else."

Seek Meaning
"When you live your purpose in-full, you achieve a life that is fulfilling, not simply time-filling."

"Faith in God and faith in Atheism are on a metaphysical par."

"That which we have carries only the value of what we gave to get it."

"Never embrace the precepts of a group wholesale, nor adopt its orthodoxy, nor follow its edicts without first testing those precepts and

orthodoxy and edicts in your own mind against alternative sources of information and insight. The question is: do YOU really think so?"

"The life lived without deep meaning cannot provide fulfillment. The life lived with meaningful purpose cannot help but deliver it."

Embrace Adversity

"It matters less how full the glass is than what it contains."

"Keeping your whine glass as empty as possible leaves room to imbibe all the other wonderful stuff of life."

"The purpose of pain is not so much to punish your actions as it is to prepare you for a better future."

"You can be a leader, if the attributes you exhibit are worth following."

"Strive for preparedness. There is no safety."

"Doing what is uncomfortable makes you more, while doing what is comfortable just makes more of you."

"We are all wounded, but you need not let your spirit be crippled. Live with the unencumbered clarity of the three-legged dog."

> *"Quote me as saying I was mis-quoted."*
>
> Groucho Marx

Notable Epigrams

JANE AUSTIN

"There are people, who the more you do for them, the less they will do for themselves."

"It isn't what we say or think that defines us, but what we do."

MATTHEW ARNOLD

"Freedom is a very good horse to ride; but to ride somewhere."

LUCILLE BALL

"In life, all good things come hard, but wisdom is the hardest to come by."

JEAN BAUDRILLARD

"Postmodernity is said to be a culture of fragmentary sensations, eclectic nostalgia, disposable simulacra, and promiscuous superficiality, in which the traditionally valued qualities of depth, coherence, meaning, originality, and authenticity are evacuated or dissolved amid the random swirl of empty signals."

SAUL BELLOW

"A great deal of intelligence can be invested in ignorance when the need for illusion is deep."

ROY T. BENNETT

"Most of us must learn to love people and use things rather than loving things and using people."

YOGI BERRA

"In theory there is no difference between theory and practice. In practice there is."

ELIZABETH BOWEN

"Childish fantasy, like the sheath over the bud, not only protects but curbs the terrible budding spirit, protects not only innocence from the world, but the world from the power of innocence."

LOUIS D. BRANDEIS

"Fear of serious injury alone cannot justify oppression of free speech and assembly. Men feared witches and burnt women. It is the function of speech to free men from the bondage of irrational fears."

"If you would only recognize that life is hard, things would be so much easier for you."

BERTOLT BRECHT

"He who fights, can lose. He who doesn't fight, has already lost."

CHARLOTTE BRONTE

"I am no bird; and no net ensnares me; I am a free human being with an independent will."

WHEN MONKEYS FLY

William C. Bryant

"These struggling tides of life that seem In wayward, aimless course to tend, Are eddies of the mighty stream That rolls to its appointed end."

Edmund Burke

"All men have equal rights, but not to equal things."

"He that struggles with us strengthens our nerves, and sharpens our skill. Our antagonist is our helper."

"Rage and frenzy will pull down more in half an hour than prudence, deliberation, and foresight can build up in a hundred years."

Leo Buscaglia

"I have a very strong feeling that the opposite of love is not hate - it's apathy. It's not giving a damn."

Albert Camus

"There is no sun without shadow, and it is essential to know the night."

Gilbert K. Chesterton

"There is a thought that stops thought. That is the only thought that ought to be stopped."

"Angels can fly because they take themselves lightly."

Dalai Lama

"The question is not to know what is the meaning of life, but what meaning I can give to my life."

"Too much self-centered attitude... brings... isolation. Result: loneliness, fear, anger. The extreme self-centered attitude is the source of suffering."

FREDERIC DOUGLAS

"There can be no independence without a large share of self-dependence"

"This virtue cannot be bestowed. It must be developed from within."

DWIGHT D. EISENHOWER

"I have always found that plans are useless, but planning is indispensable."

GEORGE ELIOT (pen name of Mary Ann Evans)

"It will never rain roses: when we want to have more roses we must plant more..."

"It is never too late to become the person you always thought you could be."

T. S. ELIOT

*"And the end of all our exploring
Will be to arrive where we started
And know the place for the first time.
Through the unknown, remembered gate
When the last of earth left to discover
Is that which was the beginning;
At the source of the longest river"*

When Monkeys Fly

Ralph Waldo Emerson

"To be yourself in a world that is constantly trying to make you something else is the greatest accomplishment."

Richard Feynman

"Science is the belief in the ignorance of experts."

Viktor Frankl

"Forces beyond your control can take away everything you possess except one thing, your freedom to choose how you will respond to the situation."

Benjamin Franklin

"Diligence is the mother of good luck."

"If everyone is thinking alike, then no one is thinking."

Mahatma Gandhi

"Honest disagreement is often a good sign of progress."

Joseph Goebbels

"If you repeat a lie often enough, people will believe it, and you will even come to believe it yourself."

Ruth Graham

"A happy marriage is the union of two good forgivers."

Lauren Green

"Don't win the argument and lose the relationship"

WERNER HEISENBERG

"The first gulp from the glass of natural sciences will turn you into an atheist, but at the bottom of the glass God is waiting for you."

CLAUDE ADRIEN HELVETIUS

"Truth is the torch that gleams through the fog without dispelling it."

ERNEST HEMMINGWAY

"Now is no time to think of what you do not have. Think of what you can do with that there is."

"There is nothing noble in being superior to your fellow men. True nobility lies in being superior to your former self."

"The world breaks everyone, and afterward, some are strong at the broken places."

ALDOUS HUXLEY

"Hell isn't merely paved with good intentions; it's walled and roofed with them. Yes, and furnished too."

WILLIAM JAMES

"A great many people think they are thinking when they are merely rearranging their prejudices."

MICHAEL JOSEPHSON

"Be thankful for quality competitors who push you to your limit."

WHEN MONKEYS FLY

FRANZ KAFKA

"It's only because of their stupidity that they're able to be so sure of themselves."

JOHN F. KENNEDY

"We must use time as a tool, not as a couch."

CHARLES KETTERING

"Every time you tear a leaf off a calendar, you present a new place for new ideas and progress."

GEORGE ROSS KIRKPATRICK

"Nature gave men two ends - one to sit on and one to think with. Ever since then man's success or failure has been dependent on the one he used most."

CHARLES KRAUTHAMMER

"Better to be paralyzed from the neck down than the neck up."

FRITZ KUNKEL

"To be mature means to face, and not evade, every fresh crisis that comes."

OSCAR LEVANT

"Underneath this flabby exterior is an enormous lack of character."

MADELEINE L'ENGLE

"... To grow up is to accept vulnerability... To be alive is to be vulnerable."

Harper Lee

"Real courage is when you know you're licked before you begin, but you begin anyway and see it through."

C. S. Lewis

"The most dangerous ideas in a society are not the ones being argued, but the ones that are assumed."

"Once people stop believing in God, the problem is not that they will believe in nothing; rather, the problem is that they will believe anything."

Myrna Loy

"Life is not a having and a getting, but a being and a becoming."

Attributed to Norm Macdonald

"How many people have to die before we finally do something about dropping pianos?"

Groucho Marx

"Those are my principles, and if you don't like them... well, I have others."

"I find television very educating. Every time somebody turns on the set, I go into the other room and read a book."

"Quote me as saying I was mis-quoted."

Cormac McCarthy

"There is no later. This is later."

WHEN MONKEYS FLY

Edward R. Murrow

"Opinions can be picked up cheap in the marketplace while such commodities as courage and fortitude and faith are in alarmingly short supply."

Friedrich Nietzsche

"Everything in the world displeases me: but, above all, my displeasure in everything displeases me."

"He who has a 'why' to live for can bear almost any 'how'."

Michael Novak

"To love is to will the good of the other, as other. Love is not restful nor sentimental in illusions, but watchful, alert, and ready to follow evidence. It seeks the real as lungs crave air."

P.J. O'Rourke

"A little government and a little luck are necessary in life, but only a fool trusts either of them."

George Orwell

"Political language… is designed to make lies sound truthful… and to give an appearance of solidity to pure wind."

Dennis Praeger

"Don't let feelings guide your behavior. Let behavior shape your feelings."

RAYMOND RADIGUET

"The source of sorrows lies not in leaving life, but in leaving that which gives it meaning."

AYN RAND

"The smallest minority on earth is the individual. Those who deny individual rights cannot claim to be defenders of minorities."

ELEANOR ROOSEVELT

"Freedom makes a huge requirement of every human being. With freedom comes responsibility. For the person who is unwilling to grow up, the person who does not want to carry his own weight, this is a frightening prospect."

GEORGE BERNARD SHAW

"A government that robs Peter to pay Paul can always depend on the support of Paul."

"This is the true joy in life... being a force of Nature instead of a feverish selfish little clod of ailments and grievances complaining that the world will not devote itself to making you happy."

"Hell is a place where you have nothing to do but amuse yourself."

SAMUEL SMILES

"Those who look into practical life will find that fortune is usually on the side of the industrious, as the winds and waves are on the side of the best navigators."

Attributed to SOCRATES

"When the debate is lost, slander becomes the tool of the loser."

WHEN MONKEYS FLY

Thomas Sowell

"Too much of what is called 'education' is little more than an expensive isolation from reality."

"The first lesson of economics is scarcity: there is never enough of anything to fully satisfy all those who want it. The first lesson of politics is to disregard the first lesson of economics."

James Surowiecki

"The important thing about groupthink is that it works not so much by censoring dissent as by making dissent seem somehow improbable."

Lionel Trilling

"We are at heart so profoundly anarchistic that the only form of state we can imagine living in is Utopian; and so cynical that the only Utopia we can believe in is authoritarian."

Mark Twain

"Some people get an education without going to college. The rest get it after they get out."

"Do something every day that you don't want to do; this is the golden rule for acquiring the habit of doing your duty without pain."

"If I cannot drink bourbon and smoke cigars in heaven, I shall not go."

Unknown

"We all get into trouble. It's how we get out of it that counts."

"Before you can achieve any goal, you must first do the one, essential thing: Name It."

"Everyone you meet is fighting a battle you know nothing about. Be Kind. Always"

"If you don't stand for something, you'll fall for anything"

OSCAR WILDE

"Be yourself; everyone else is taken."

FRANK YERBY

"Maturity is reached the day we don't need to be lied to about anything."

INDEX

Prolog.. 1
Introduction 3
Contents 11
FLIGHTS 18
   Think and Speak for Yourself... 19
Medieval Torture of the Mind 21
Invasion of the Pod People 25
Virtually Tribal 27
Visit Hypnotic Stockholm 30
Of Toddlers and Bigots 33
Intellectual Suicide 33
Ideological Segregationists 36
The Super-Collider 39
Be Disagreeable 41
Uncivil Projectiles 42
Think and Speak for Yourself 43
   Choose Freedom Over Comfort 47
The Unruly 49
No Slave to Robots 53
Bleeding to Death 59
Equality of Misery 61
The Pie Fight 63
Drifting Free 66
Phone Dead 68
Playing Monopoly 69

The Shell Game	72
The Free Market Escalator	74
Choose Freedom Over Comfort	76
Own Your Outcomes	81
Honkers	83
Tack	85
Mountaineering	86
Dirty Fingernails	88
Itemized Bills	90
Beware Ease	93
Safety Chains	95
Killing Monsters	97
Minding Weeds	98
Fixing Things	100
Letting Fly	102
No Past Future	104
No Biting	106
When Would Now be a Good Time?	108
24	110
Own Your Outcomes	112
Be Skeptical	115
Drunk at the Wheel	117
The Rule of Exceptions	121
On the Other Hand	123
Shepherds	126
Privileged to Build Here	128
Lawyer-up	130

Runners 133
Dead Certain 134
Be Skeptical 135
    Confront Fashionable Nonsense 139
The Postmodern Abyss 141
Newspeak 2 143
Self-immolation 157
Confront Fashionable Nonsense 159
    Put Away Childish Things 163
Of Copernicus and Youth 164
Fixing Flats 166
Failure to Molt 169
Passionately Incompetent 171
Of Pride and Pretense 173
Peter Pan on Campus 175
Theoretically Infatuated 177
When It's Not Academic 178
The Unschooled Harvest 179
It's Concerning 180
Cold Water 181
A Torch to Carry 182
Put Away Childish Things 184
    Treasure Individuals 187
Abusing Demographics 189
Beyond Average 192
Do Judge 194
Tight Lipped 196

Good for Who?	197
Unlovable Neighbors	198
The Greater Angel of Relationship	199
Personally Apolitical	200
Love of Words	202
Marital Glue	202
When "Yes" Means "Yes"	203
Opening Doors	204
Treasure Individuals	205
Live Consciously	209
Spending Time with Zombies	211
Chewing Gum	213
Pull the Plug	215
Moo	217
Indigestion	220
Time-share Contracts	220
Selfie-stuck	222
The Price of Exhilaration	223
Salted Caramel	223
Live Consciously	225
Seek Meaning	229
On Purpose	231
Arc of Life	233
Uniquely Meaningful	235
A Stool to Stand On	237
Keeping What You Give	239
Taking a Ride	240

The Atheist's Catch 22	241
A Serene End	244
A Dignified End	245
The Material Lens	246
Seek Meaning	248
Embrace Adversity	251
Whine Glasses	253
Losing Winners	254
Batter Up	256
Unsafe Spaces	257
Prepare for Courage	259
More of You	260
Getting There	262
Too Hard Not To	263
Pivot to Success	264
Leading Attributes	265
Embrace Adversity	266
Epilogue	269
BAGGAGE CLAIM	272
A Monkey Made Me Do It	273
Flying Monkeys?	274
Footnote	274
From the Author	275
Attribution	276
Thanks	276
Author's Quotes	277
Notable Epigrams	286

INDEX 298

Made in the USA
Middletown, DE
04 June 2025

76529739R00170